Epiphanies Within

When Mediocre Living Is
No Longer Enough

Brittney Michelle

Unless otherwise indicated, all Scripture quotations are taken from the Holy Bible, King James Version (Public Domain).

ISBN-13: 978-0-9863813-1-7

Contact Information:

For more information about scheduling the author for a seminar or book discounts please contact the author at the email provided: contactme@itsbrittneymichelle.com.

BM Webster Publishing, LLC

http://www.itsBrittneyMichelle.com

Dedication

First and Foremost, I give all glory and honor to my Lord and Savior Jesus Christ. He is my Source, and without Him, I am nothing. There are no words in the English language that can express just how thankful I am for His grace, mercy, and favor.

I dedicate this book to my Father, my Mother, and my two younger brothers: Michael and Joshua, and to all of my loving family and friends who have supported me as I follow my dreams. Thank you all for believing in me, for supporting me, for sacrificing for me, and for constantly reminding me that I am destined to be great. I am blessed beyond measure to have each and every one of you in my life. I promise to make you all proud.

Table of Contents:

Introduction

I am a young woman traveling through one of the most vital stages of my life to date: the journey that leads from the post teenage/college years, to real life, full blown adulthood.

As a recent college graduate, I definitely have a long way to go before I can consider myself a true "grown woman," however, the experiences I've gone through, as well as the many observations I've made of those closest to me, have inspired me to write this book. I wanted to take the time to speak directly from my heart; to help the countless young ladies out there who are just like me, struggling to balance this thing called life.

Let's face it, women are complicated. There usually isn't just one part of our lives that seems to be going haywire at one time: it's actually more like five, six, or seven parts. It is not unusual for it to feel as if once one part of our life flies out of whack, everything else immediately follows. Well, I'm no different than you are; which is why I've channeled my assorted thoughts and experiences into this one book, or what I like to call a multi-topical collection of eye opening advice. Whether it be guys and relationships, emotions, future careers, or finding your God-given purpose, this book will cover it all.

Now, let me forewarn you, this is not your average "self-help" book. I believe that every girl's journey to womanhood is different; therefore, there is no set guideline on how to do it "right." I cannot give you a guaranteed step-by-step tutorial to magically eliminate every problem in your life, nor can I claim to know it all. I can only offer *my* advice based on my own personal knowledge and experiences. I feel like open-ended advice is the best type of advice because you are able to apply it to your own life. Open-ended advice is specific enough to strike a nerve, causing you to recognize parallels that exist between you and topic of discussion, while at the same time vague enough as to give you room to apply it to the very personal details of your own experiences. The same methods don't work the same for everyone, so this type of advice simply opens your mind to what only you can discover for yourself.

Hopefully, my words will shed light on your situations and offer a bit of encouragement and wisdom so that you don't have to learn every lesson the hard way. Use this book as a guide towards a new way of thinking! It is my hope that reading these words will force you to ask yourself a few questions about your current state and the direction in which your life is headed.

On the journey to womanhood, our minds develop into something we never imagined when we were younger. As you begin to mature in various areas, you tend to look deeper into "life" and analyze the world and the people around you in different ways. Some things that once seemed so simple may now seem far more complex. Emotions that never existed now seem to take over your whole being. Some days you may feel lost and confused about just about everything spanning from what you want to do professionally to who you really are as a person. I want to assure you that not only are these uncomfortable growing pains natural, but they are healthy and imperative for growth. It takes awhile for a person to come into form, mentally, physically, spiritually, etc. So don't be afraid. Being a woman is hard work! Just know you are not alone.

It is my hope and prayer that after reading this book, you will understand the importance of gaining control of your mind and your emotions, while learning just how much the way you choose to look at the world can affect your day-to-day life experiences.

Don't feel bad if you don't have the answers to all of the questions or problems that life throws your way. Life got a whole lot easier for me when I realized that everything isn't always black and white. The answer isn't always as clear as day and there isn't always a sign to tell us which way to go. Sometimes, the answer is somewhere in the middle. I think the solutions to life's deepest questions are often found along the journey. The journey makes us who we are. Without the journey, we wouldn't gain the perspective needed to tell our story in the way God wants us to tell it. It's the hardships, the troubles and the struggle that make the story worthwhile. In order to see the beauty in the pain and use your trials for greatness, you must first learn to recognize a lesson when it's staring you in the face. Internal growth can be a difficult reality to endure, but it's a process we should embrace with open arms. I am so appreciative of each and every lesson in maturity, what I have come to see as epiphanies within.

Epiphany 1

You have to be completely honest with yourself and figure out who YOU really are...

"I'm Starting With The Man In The Mirror ... I'm Asking Him To Change His Ways...." – **Michael Jackson**

"You have to get to know yourself." How many times have we all heard that one? If you were anything like me, then you'd agree that this statement sounded pretty absurd at first. I mean, seriously, how and why would I need to get to know myself? I am ME, who could possibly know more about who I am than ME? These are questions I couldn't quite wrap my head around when I first heard those words. The truth of the matter, however, is that they are 100 percent true and one of the most important things a girl must do before she can truly embrace both womanhood and herself. The same goes for a boy becoming a man, but we're not talking about them right now.

Let me attempt to break it down for you. A girl grows up with her parents (or whatever familial structure it may be); consequently a huge bulk of her identity is tied up in that familial unit. She thinks the way they think; believes in what they believe in; eats what they eat; runs a household the way they've taught her to, etc. Yes, there are some differences here and there, seeing that everyone ultimately has their own personality, but more often than not, a young person is a reflection of the home and community they grew up in. When that same girl leaves home for the first time and goes off on her own, to college for example, she is exposed to a new and different way of life.

When I got to college, I realized so much about myself within the first two years alone. It was the first time I was exposed to people outside of my family twenty-four hours a day, seven days a week. It was the little things that got me, like how my roommates' grocery shopped for different types of food than my mom did. Although that may sound very small or insignificant, it made me realize how closed the box I was living in had been my entire life —as many of us have. I grew up doing things in my parents' household a particular way and had never even thought to do them any differently until I was out on my own and making my own decisions. I'd come home and my friends or family would notice these changes and say, "When did you start eating that?" or, "Since when do you do that?" Some of these decisions were as tiny and minute as what brand of laundry detergent to purchase, while others were bigger decisions like what type of church I wanted to attend.

The point I'm trying to make here is that we often get so settled in a routine, but don't always notice it. Consequently, the routine becomes a big part of who we think we are, not because we've made those conscious decisions for ourselves, but because someone told us that's how things should go and we rolled with it. I believe that is why people are so quick to judge others and throw the "you've changed" card when they go and return from college. Sometimes it's not that the person has "changed" like a chameleon adapting to their surroundings, but that they are finally in a position where they must discover who they really are and what they really like to do with their time, money, feelings and friends.

If I look back at who I was at 17 or 18, although I am still the same Brittney, I can barely recognize myself in some ways. If you ever doubt the fact that you've changed over the last five years or so, just take a stroll down memory lane via your Facebook profile and you'll be amazed by how far you've come. Seriously, I took a stroll down memory lane; circa 2007 Facebook statuses and, umm, yea, totally embarrassed.

It takes a lot of self-confidence to be yourself. Even more importantly, it takes progression and maturity to recognize when who you're trying to be every day is not the real you. Now, you're probably thinking, "Okay so how do I do that? How do I get to 'know myself' before it's too late? How do I take proactive steps to get to know me before I end up looking back on another set of Facebook pictures and statuses saying to myself, 'Who did I think I was?'" Well, for me personally, I believe that the first step must be strengthening your everyday relationship with God. You will find that once you spend honest, tangible time getting to know Him, He will in turn show you, you! That's a pretty hefty concept that we'll touch on in a chapter to come.

I've also found that journaling is one of the best ways to "get to know yourself." Whether it is video diaries like the one Beyoncé did for her 2013 documentary, "Life is but a Dream"; random notes in your phone; or an old school diary, try to get your thoughts out so that you can look back on them in some way or another! It's dangerous to keep your thoughts bottled up in your head. Not only because you can become emotionally stifled, but because you often forget the issue and what you learned from it once it's over. When you start to feel better (temporarily), you tend to quickly forget the pain you were feeling, therefore, never properly dealing with the issues... and we all know what happens when you throw salt on a wound that hasn't healed properly.

That is why I am constantly writing things down. The notes section in my phone is filled with hundreds of random notes of frustration and emotion, prayer requests, and bursts of energy and confidence when I feel like God reveals something great to me. I know how it is for a lot of girls; you finally wind down from a long day and get in your bed to go to sleep and you can't. Why? Because you get stuck in your feelings, thinking about any and everything that went wrong today, yesterday, or last year. All you want to do is sleep and forget about everything, but you can't because your mind and emotions want to have a field day all night long. The joys of being a girl, right?

I've come to realize that sometimes being alone and in your feelings can actually be a great thing in retrospect. When you're all wrapped up in your emotions and there is nobody else around to judge you is when you're at your most vulnerable point. You aren't prideful, or trying to be a "big girl," you're just sensitive and open. That is usually when your heart speaks the clearest.

Write down everything you're feeling and why you feel that way. It therapeutically allows your mind to process what exactly is wrong, release it from your brain, and hopefully fall asleep. When things start to get better, or you have a "light bulb moment" jot that down too! You'd be surprised to see how often we go through the same tests and trials over and over again and still can't get them right because we don't recognize that we've been there before. How can you learn from your mistakes if you don't even remember them? Same situation, different guy...or similar problem, different circumstances.

When you journal through your issues, you can look back and say, "Okay, I've been here before. I cried over him for weeks and now he barely crosses my mind, so I know I can move on again—I know there will be other guys." Or, "I felt like a failure when I was going through this the last time because of how negatively I was thinking about the situation--let me not do that this time."

Sometimes you've just got to check yourself, REAL QUICK! You know how you are, so you know that certain thoughts will have you, A) thinking too hard about things you cannot control, or B) having a pity party. I'm that girl, I'm very emotional. I don't always show it, but the emotions are there. I constantly have to tell myself to "chill" because I refuse to allow fickle emotions to control me. They'll try to destroy you if you let them. In all honesty, you know what makes you tick, and sometimes you just don't even need to let yourself go there. Learn to counsel yourself! Despite how difficult it may be, sometimes you have to force yourself to stop feeling bad about your current situation. Self-pity has never gotten anyone anywhere, ever... Well, at least not anywhere I'm trying to go. At times you're blessed to have someone encourage you when things get rough, but most times you have to learn to reach deep down inside and find that voice that is able to speak life against the spirit of discouragement. Being your own cheering squad isn't easy, but I've learned it's the best one you could ever have!

In a nutshell, you have to figure out what it is that YOU are doing that is keeping you in the same cycle. You can't get out of the imprisonment that is your own mind until you discover that you're imprisoned in the first place.

So, the next time you hear someone say the term "getting to know yourself," try to think of it more as a healthy, deep thinking process. Think of it as taking the time out to figure out exactly how you process situations, not how people tell you that you should process them. What works for someone else's life may not work for yours, but you won't know that until you pay attention to the details of your own being.

How do major companies find out what business tools or marketing strategies are more successful than others? They record data and make changes accordingly. You are no different! Mirror checks are powerful!

Epiphany 2

Learn From Your Mistakes.
Grow From Your Heartaches.

"We live in a generation of,
not being in love, and not being together.
But we still make it feel like we're together,
Cause we're scared to see each other with somebody else." - ***Drake***

Men, you can't live with them, and you can't live without them. Well, that's how the saying goes anyway. I can almost guarantee that a large majority of every woman's concern in life starts with those three letters, M-E-N. They have the ability to drive us crazy; make us smile; fall in love; hurt our feelings all in the same day. Trust me ladies, I know! I sometimes wonder, "Do women ever take the time to think about how much control they really give men over their lives?"

If you're anything like I was about two years ago, you probably will answer that question by saying, "I'm independent and I know what I want in a man. I won't settle for anything less than the best!" Meanwhile, you're constantly in a feud or lover's quarrel with an ex, "boo," or "lover & friend", and don't even realize the amount of wear and tear you're putting your mind, heart and emotions through.

Now, first things first. I never thought of myself as a girl who had been damaged by love or relationships, mainly because I'd been single, or so I thought, pretty much my entire collegiate career. I couldn't relate to most of the relationship advice I'd heard or been given, because in my mind, none of it applied to a single lady like myself. It wasn't until my fifth and final year of college that I finally realized I had a problem or two. I realized that I was scared of relationships in their entirety. Scared to be vulnerable. Scared of what I thought was love, and what it could do. Scared to trust someone enough to believe they really cared about me. Scared to actually admit to being wide open. I had let fear get me to the point of allowing "situationships," as many people like to call them, to harden my heart to the point that I barely even recognized myself.

So... The first step to fixing a problem is acknowledging that there is a problem in the first place. First, I realized I was a serial situationship dater. A situationship is not a relationship with an official title, but a situation involving two people who are operating as if they are in a relationship, with relationship type issues and drama. The word situationship is a widely spreading term that has become quite popular among this generation. (Even though I SWEAR I thought I made it up. Ha-ha; that is until I heard my peers, and even rapper, Fabolous, reference it in one of one of his songs.) Generally speaking, situationships are usually fragile and very messy because there is little room for rules and boundaries, leaving ample space and opportunity for pride and damaged feelings.

Situationships are very common among the college population for many reasons. You see, the high school guys who were so eager to "love," have a girlfriend, and settle down, arrive in college suffering from the fact that the only girl they feel they will ever truly love broke their hearts at age 17. (I know you've all met *that* guy.) Needless to say, those guys are now ready to explore the jungle that is college with no strings attached.

Then you have the young college girls who don't know how to handle this new breed of young men, but are so desperate for attention that they'll just take what they can get, even if that means no title. I mean, in high school every other boy you knew had a girlfriend. Now, you get to college and all of a sudden, they all want to be single? Did anybody else miss the memo, or was that just me? So, needless to say, we're cool with it, holding the thought in mind that we'll wear him down, and eventually he'll be practically begging us for the title! (Once he sees how absolutely awesome we are, right?)

The fact of the matter is, situationships can cause just as much, if not more, damage as a committed relationship. In a committed relationship, a couple has established rules and boundaries— lines that cannot be crossed without repercussions. They give each other "titles," like, "You're my boyfriend. You're my girlfriend." There is a great sense of security in knowing that each partner publicly claims their unwavering commitment for each other.

The opposite is often true in a situationship where two people may claim to "not be looking for a relationship" for whatever reason, so they play the game without the necessary protocol for an intentional courtship. There is often so much grey area in a situationship, that people find themselves in awkward predicaments that they aren't sure how to solve or remove themselves from. It's always easy to fall back on the "Well, I'm not your girlfriend," or "He isn't officially mine" excuses. In some cases, two people get it together and a situationship leads to a boyfriend/girlfriend relationship. However, in most cases, people find themselves "talking," whatever that really means, for lengths of time— which often backfires in one way or another.

I strongly believe that you have at least three options when something goes badly, in anything in life, but especially in a romantically charged situation. One, you can examine what happened, where it went wrong and how it affected you, then chalk it up as a learning experience. Or, option two, you can feel sorry for yourself and carry the baggage with you from one situation to the next. Option three, you can stay stuck in a situation because no matter how painful it may be, it's what you're used to.

I know what you're probably thinking; you don't have any baggage right? Well, baggage can simply be a defense mechanism we develop over time. More often than not, we don't know how to take the first option, because we are blinded by our emotions. Nine times out of ten, when my emotions are tied-up in something, it's impossible to think rationally and logically. When I say impossible, I really mean impossible. Have you ever been so extremely upset by something your "boo" or boyfriend did that you acted out of character? Of course you have. We all have. Now, how did you feel after it was all over, let's say a week or so later? You probably couldn't believe you let something get to you so much to the point that it affected your behavior. Oh, not you huh? So you didn't delete his number, delete all his calls out of your call history, AND the text message threads in an angry fit of rage? Or what about the time you wasted all those precious hours pouting all day, listening to sad love songs, mad at the world because of what he did? Emotions have the ability to take us places, mentally, that make us feel beside ourselves. As a result, we end up taking the more dangerous routes— options two or three.

I, like most, am guilty of doing so. By the time I realized I had the whole "scared of relationships" syndrome, I had collected so much baggage over the years that it all began to pile up. If you have not heard it before, let me be the first to tell you, to go from thinking you are perfectly fine, to realizing you are an emotional volcano ready to erupt, to sorting out and dealing with your issues, is an emotionally draining experience.

It began when I enrolled in a course for college women taught by my pastor's wife, First Lady Erica Glenn (Lady E.), of my home church, Revolution Christian Ministries (Grand Rapids, MI). Lady E told us that the course would change our lives, but like most of the others, I wasn't totally convinced at first. My life seemed to be going just fine, and although I didn't have a boyfriend, I figured it was because all the guys around me were fools and too immature to appreciate a good girl like me.

On the first day of class, she suggested that in order to completely gain all that we could from the course, we'd need to go on a "man-fast." Basically, in a nutshell, the man-fast was a 30-day long halt from all communication with men. That meant any man that we were currently or had ever been romantically interested in, had to be cut off, for a whole month. I can't lie; I struggled with my decision to participate. I had never heard of anything of the sort and I didn't see the purpose of doing it, particularly considering that I was single.

I faced an internal battle as I decided whether or not I wanted to participate in the class. Then it hit me. I literally asked myself, "If I'm single, with no boyfriend, meaning no one is committed to me, then why am I struggling with the decision at all?" I had no good answer to that question. Once I realized I was even remotely contemplating risking an opportunity to better my relationship with God and learn more about myself, for the sake of talking to a few guys that I already knew weren't MINE, I recognized a problem. I started asking myself, "Why not do it? What am I worried about?"

At that very moment, I had a huge revelation. It was then that I realized that the main reason I'd been avoiding the fast was because I feared the unknown. I wasn't sure how my "boo's" would react when I told them I couldn't talk to them for a month. Even worse, I worried that they'd move on to someone else during the time I was "away." As I said before, none of these "boo's" I had at the time were in a relationship with me, so in reality, I had nothing at all to lose. I was disappointed in myself once I realized my reasoning for not wanting to do something so positive for myself was based on the thoughts, actions, and feelings of other people.

At that point I made up my mind that I was going to do the fast and not look back. I wasn't sure what issues I had to deal with, but I knew that I wanted to regain the peace of mind I once had. Deep in my heart I knew something wasn't right. I just couldn't pinpoint what it was or where it started, but I knew that my overall joy was at an all-time low.

This was the beginning of my journey towards a healthier heart. In order to understand my revelations, you must first know my story. It isn't anything completely drastic or heart wrenching. I didn't find out my boyfriend was cheating on me with my best friend or anything that extreme, which is probably why I never realized I had any issues. I mean, I didn't even have a boyfriend, so how could I have relationship scars when I hadn't even been in a relationship in a while? I'm sure you're probably curious to know what I gained from this "man-fast." Well, I can honestly say that it changed my life by putting a lot of things into perspective, thus redirecting me away from a path of emotional stress and strain.

Although the fast only lasted thirty days, the revelations, knowledge and healing I gained during that time were only a spark that led to the real process, which was the restoration of my emotions and the acknowledgement of my worth. In the end, it was more than worth it, but it was hard. Loneliness is a feeling that most of us are not capable of handling at first. However, I realized that when you're alone with yourself, you're able to see things that you can't see when others are constantly around. You have time to think through issues that you don't have time to think about when you're on the phone flirting with your crush all night. When you're forced to be lonely, you can't blame your feelings on anyone else. You can't look to someone else to make you happy. Ultimately, I realized that "lonely" isn't so bad when it serves a purpose. The class forced me to take a look at my own biggest enemy, the only person that was truly holding me back.... *Myself.*

After examining the characteristics of the various dating situations I was involved in, I noticed a pattern. The pattern, like I said before, being complex feelings, without always having instituted boyfriend/girlfriend titles in the relationship. Situationships. While it is important to "name" your relationship, so as to establish boundaries and commitment, the heart doesn't need these titles for feelings to develop. So, as I downplayed and overlooked the scars I received from these "situations," which were indeed "relationships" in their own right, my heart was slowly getting colder and colder. I think it's important for women to know that heart damage comes in many different shapes and sizes. You cannot minimize the pain you feel because it doesn't seem as bad as the next person's. Pain is pain, and no matter how deep the cut, it still hurts.

Like most girls, I hardly ever looked at what I did to make my relationships or situationships crumble. I also failed to realize that sometimes, I just needed to remove myself altogether. I always chalked it up to men being stupid! During my mental vacation away from men, I started to realize that, perhaps, I not only contributed to the problems I'd experienced, but added fuel to the fire, either passively or actively.

As I share this advice with you, I'm not going to go into EVERY single miniscule detail of what happened between each guy and I, or every little thing they may have done to hurt me. Why? Because at the end of the day, we've all heard those sob stories before. There will be guys who will continue to make dumb decisions and hurt girls that care about them until the day the earth is no more (and vice versa). It's life. Don't like the way this sounds? Bear with me and just let me explain. While immature people will continue to do what they do, you have the power to decide what you will and will not put up with. You have the power to speak up when you don't like how someone is acting. You also have the power to walk away when the person you're dealing with doesn't respect and honor the valuable treasure that YOU are.

You owe it to yourself to turn every heartache you feel into a learning experience that makes you grow into the dynamic woman God created you to be. It's time we stop blaming men for the way we feel about love and relationships. I think we, as woman, are often too quick to do that. We'd rather feel sorry for ourselves than forgive, grow, and become better. Hurt people, hurt people. If you allow yourself to wallow in your hurt, you may end up hurting the one guy who's different from all the rest. It's time to woman-up and accept our role in the viscous cycle and work to break out from it.

After it's all said and done, I have nothing bad to say about any of the four guys I am about to mention. They aren't the only guys I've ever dated or "talked to" in my life, but these are the four that I feel had the greatest impact and resulted in the biggest lessons learned during the time span covered in this book. Over the years, I've been able to reconcile and forgive them all, so I don't want anyone to mistake me telling my stories as me bashing them or "throwing shade" (publically criticizing them.) In all honesty, it's not even about them! It's about me. Well actually, it's about you too,

US...because I know I'm not the only one who's been in similar situations. At the end of the day, I'm glad to say that I can actually consider a couple of them my friends now.

By no means am I perfect. Just as I've been hurt, I know I've hurt a few along the way as well. However, the most important thing I've taken from my past is the ability to look between the lines, and pull out the valuable lessons from between the waves of the storm. As humans we are flawed, but sometimes our flaws are used to change the lives of others.

One of the major faults I noticed when examining my choices with guys, is the fact that I'd literally jump from one relationship or situationship to the next, without giving myself time to recover and even process what went wrong. I started off as a naïve girl who wore her heart right on her sleeve.

During my late teen years I was in puppy love—in a two-year off and on relationship with guy #1—which ended on not so good terms due to a combination of the immaturities of the both of us. The baggage I carried from the failure of this relationship was the inability to see my own faults. I never stopped to realize that maybe I was immature and picked some of the fights that were taking place. That maybe I didn't appreciate the times he tried to be a great boyfriend, because I was too busy worrying about what my "friends" thought of him, which came about from me always venting about the negatives, but keeping to myself all the good things. Looking back, I now see that through all of our ups and downs, he was without doubt a good guy that I learned a lot from. He'd say the same about me now, but back then neither of us really appreciated each other. We didn't quite realize so until years later as we mended our friendship and reflected on the past.

Don't get me wrong, everything wasn't always good and gravy, especially in the beginning of our relationship. There were many times when he made me so mad that I wanted to call my friends and pop up at his house or job and do damage. I let it bring out the worst in me sometimes; even to the point of getting into altercations with a few girls. (So immature, right?) Things got extremely childish and petty on both our parts; the evidence is still probably on our Facebook pages somewhere.

As the smoke cleared I never knew how to forgive, even though he was able to forgive me for my part in the drama that we had. Instead, I tried to venture out and explore the beginning of college life; all while knowing he was still at home in case the grass wasn't really greener on the other side. He did the same thing, but he usually tried a little harder than I did to make it work. Eventually, I think, I subconsciously pushed him away until he had no choice but to move on. In actuality, we couldn't really offer what each other needed at the time, and we began to outgrow one another. Once that happened, instead of seeing things clearly, I carried this idea that someone who claimed to be down for me, would eventually, in time, walk away and leave me alone. The moral of the story is, if you don't appreciate someone while they're good to you, you cannot be mad when they decide to be good to someone else.

After that, there I was, eager to find a replacement. I was so used to having that one person, and was so darn bored by myself, that I didn't know how to function alone. There I was, on the rebound, spending all my time with guy #2. Thus starting the ever-so-destructive habit of carrying baggage from one situation to the next. I went into this new situation with the idea that guys were not supportive or loyal. I figured that if I showed too much emotion, he'd gain some power over me that I didn't want him to have. So I put up emotional walls and acted like nothing he did affected me, good or bad. I was not the nonchalant type in the beginning, but for some reason, I started to pretend to be that way. Let me assure you, if you start playing a role long enough, eventually that role becomes hard to separate from your actual self.

I'll never doubt the fact that this guy actually cared about me. If anyone ever has, I know he did. He never shied away from showing so, even to this day. However, I was so "anti-relationships" by the time we got serious, that I wasn't willing to take that risk again. So, I played the tough girl role until it smacked me right in the face. I figured that if we kept this thing going, at strictly the situationship level, then he could never hurt me or get to my emotions.

After about a year or so, things got shaky between this guy and me. That usually happens when two people haven't established clear lines of where exactly they're headed, and to be honest, I didn't even know where I wanted it to go. It was mid-college, I was "doing me," just enjoying the college life, and he was doing the same; so whatever it was that we had seemed to *work*. Initially we argued occasionally, which turned to more frequently, and then a huge bomb was dropped when I found out that everyone else but me knew he was still involved with his ex- girlfriend. He hadn't been honest with me about this fact, so I felt like a "side chick" after finding out. As if my emotional walls weren't already high enough, they inched up a little higher after that. My pride and emotional disconnect wouldn't allow me to show that I was affected by it. So, I held all of my feelings of embarrassment, disappointment, and betrayal inside. Despite his countless acts of kindness and sincere apologies, I didn't let things get back to how they used to be between us. At the time, I guess I kept thinking, "Here we go again... déjà vu," so my defensive instincts made me shut down. Even still, over the years he never stopped apologizing and showing that he genuinely cared about me as a person. We worked through our issues time after time, and years later, he still has my back. I'll always appreciate him for that, because to me, that's what it's all about. Just because two people don't work out in a relationship, doesn't mean they have to end up hating each other. Sometimes it ends like that, but I think it says a lot when you can learn from what the two of you had, put the ill feelings behind you, and move on.

So anyway, within about a month and a half of things falling apart with guy #2, I bounced right under the spell of guy #3, expecting him to take away the pain of the last. I've realized that the majority of my issues with the idea of relationships started here. This one was what most girls like me would consider a "very good guy." He was very active in his church, and stayed on me about doing so as well, had a good head on his shoulders, good communicator, and had great goals. He was straight up and didn't beat around the bush about his intentions to see us in a relationship sooner than later. That won me over right away, because suddenly, a committed relationship sounded appealing to me. My "no strings attached" method hadn't played out too well, so I decided that this time around would have to involve commitment. Basically, he seemed like the total package. Mind you, I'd had a run in with him a few years back that should've forewarned me of what he was capable of (disappearing), but like most girls, I ignored the signs and figured he had matured and changed by now. In my mind, I figured that the reason guy #2 ended up messing around with his ex was because he and I were always getting into an argument about one thing or another. Most people dislike like catty women. So this time around, I took the calm, cool and collected approach.

This guy and I didn't argue, not because he did everything perfectly and I didn't have anything to complain about, but because I kept my mouth shut in fear that he'd think I was too much of a nagger and move on to the next girl. I didn't realize that's what I was doing at the time, but in retrospect, it's all very obvious now. By ignoring the small stuff and letting him get away with things that should have been corrected, I handed him the power over our relationship on a platter. He knew that he could do whatever he wanted within reason and I wouldn't say anything, because I was the nice girl. I couldn't even see that I was ultimately hurting myself, because I was too busy worrying if he was good.

You can't be so afraid of losing someone's company that you lose the ability to stand up for yourself. When you start to notice that you're sacrificing your own complete happiness for the sake of someone else's feelings, or to avoid a reaction, you need to stop and ask yourself how much you really value yourself? A person will only treat you as well as you treat yourself. If you act like it's no big deal when they do things that are really eating you up inside, you're pretty much telling them that you're completely okay with the way they're treating you. Professional Life Coach Tony Gaskins said it best, "You teach people how to treat you by what you allow, what you stop, and what you reinforce."

Eventually, things fell apart with that dysfunctional love affair and he disappeared. Literally. We went from 100-to-0 in one day. He just stopped answering the phone and I couldn't find him anywhere. I mean, how do you explain that to people? How do you explain that to yourself? I'm no rocket scientist, but I don't think it's a coincidence that this happened on the very day that the word virgin came up in conversation. I don't really know the right words to describe how it feels to have a person you think you're building something with just completely cut you off with no word or warning, but what comes to mind is: bamboozled. He resurfaced about seven months later, claiming that I was his soul mate. I reluctantly attempted to give "us" another try, only because he begged and convinced me that things would be different. However, like clockwork, within a few months he walked away again, deciding that being with me was not where he wanted to be. Talk about confusing, right?

"Mental note: This is EXACTLY why you're not supposed to let your guard down..." I told myself.

So there I was, a young college girl who in reality, really hadn't spent more than 60 days "alone" in the past four years, dealing with issues and bottled up emotions from three different situations. I didn't think I could do any wrong and that I just had horrible luck with guys. I had an emotional wall built up that told me that a man would lie to me, cheat on me, and make me look like a fool if I ever acted like I cared about him. I felt like I had to accept the dumb things men did because if not, I'd be too much of a nagger. I had faulty evidence to validate why I had become so close-hearted in the first place, and convinced myself that caring for someone, even a little bit would always get thrown back in my face. To top it all off, I was actually a bit ashamed of my virginity all because one person decided that it was too much of a liability rather than an asset. Crazy right? Looking back, he actually did me a favor. I didn't see it that way back then though and since I never took the time to acknowledge these issues and process what was going on, I couldn't break the cycle. These emotions were subconsciously building off each other, creating more and more damage.

That following summer I decided that relationships were out of the question for me. I was tired of getting my feelings hurt. Tired of getting caught up, only for everything to come crashing down. I tried to "Think Like A Man, and ACT like one too." I purposely entertained as many guy "friends" as I could find. I wasn't acting like my normal self because I was hurt, and I was confused. The moment I felt I was spending too much time with one particular guy, I'd drop him and switch over to another. My vision was so cloudy I couldn't even see that I was playing a guy to the left, who was actually trying to get to know me. I guess that's what recording artist, Big Sean meant when he said "what's the perfect girl if it's not the perfect time?" If someone's mind isn't in the right place, there's almost nothing you can say/do to change that. I wasn't looking for anything serious, nothing long term. At least that's what I told myself, and well, that would be how I found myself in this final situationship.

To make a long story short: Girl and Boy are really good friends throughout every situation I previously mentioned. However, over the years and throughout their own various relationships and situationships, boy and girl have started to develop feelings for one another. Unfortunately, boy has a whole lot of trust issues. Girl has significant baggage. Boy and girl cross the imaginary line that exists between friends and more than friends. Nothing is ever the same. But, they're such close friends that no matter how complicated things get, they rarely go more than a day without speaking to each other. They just can't seem to figure out what position they want to play in one another's lives. However, most days, they claim to be just friends. Eventually, that starts to get old and emotions do what they do best. Complicate things.

Girl tries to cut emotional ties. Boy convinces girl to stay around and trust him. Girl stays around and trusts him. Things seem to be going pretty well, until boy shows signs that indicate he's not as serious with girl as she'd hoped he was. Girl tries to walk away to avoid getting hurt. Boy spills his heart out and makes it seem like maybe there is hope for them after all. He's able to sell the story that they will actually be able to make something work in the near future, but that he just doesn't think a relationship would be best at the current time. Girl is hopeful, excited, and worried; yet too emotionally invested to lose him, so she continues to play both the friend and the "boo" roles, depending on the day of the week. After all, girl feels it is better to spend time with someone she is confident will never hurt her, despite the lack of a "title," than risk trying to open up with anyone else. Then, out of the blue, boy pops up with a new girlfriend. Surprise!

I promise if you just listen to the lyrics in Musiq Soulchild's "Half Crazy" and then Destiny Child's "Is She The Reason" you'll completely understand what I was going through. This situation hurt me the most because it was a totally different feeling. I was wide open. I wasn't hiding anything, or pretending, or trying to avoid getting hurt. There was no such thing as having my guard up with him, because at the end of the day we had been friends for several years. He knew me better than any other guy, and I knew him better than any other girl.

Or so I thought. Until then, I didn't know how it felt to have someone claim that no matter what, they'd never do anything to hurt you, do the complete opposite of everything they'd ever promised. I never expected to be caught off guard like that. Sure I'd had my feelings hurt in the past, but it didn't compare to this one.

For some reason, I put him on a pedestal and foolishly never even thought he'd come down. So now, on top of all the other issues I held internally, I was completely embarrassed and devastated (or at least it felt that way at the time). Ultimately, the worst part was not that he had found a girlfriend. When you really care for someone, you want him or her to be happy—even if it means with someone other than you. The part that hurt my feelings the most, the part that haunted me for so long, was that I had lost who I felt was my closest male friend, confidant, and person to talk to at any time of the day or night. Not only that, he quite frankly, really didn't seem to miss me not one bit. In all honesty, what really got me, was that I finally realized that as much as I cared about him as a person and friend, in the end, it wasn't mutual. I was mad at myself. Mad for being played. Mad that I was tricked and fooled. Mad that I missed all the signs. Mad that I didn't beat him to the punch.

Sometimes it takes pain to snap you into reality and force a wake-up call; to put an end to a vicious cycle that is breaking you down time after time again. If it didn't hurt so bad, you'd never walk away. Now, I must add that the man-fast happened in the midst of this last situation. It actually happened somewhere around the, "Boy shows signs that indicate he's not as serious with girl as she hoped he'd be" part of the story. It was here that I was able to pinpoint the many issues I'd left unresolved over the years and the domino effect they had on each subsequent interaction. Once I realized what I was doing to myself time after time, I made a conscious effort to do better. I realized that as much as I said I valued myself and as much as I claimed to believe I deserved a guy that would treat me like a queen, my actions proved otherwise. I had allowed myself to get attached to situations that did not have the proper structure in the first place. God must come first. Rules and boundaries must be established. Transparency in regards to feelings/emotions is crucial. Finally, both parties need a clear, mutual understanding of what direction they'd like to see their relationship head over time. I'd made none of these things a priority, and I finally realized that the madness had to cease.

After a lot of prayer and self-reflection, I felt a huge weight being lifted off my shoulders. I was ready to start brand new! Hence; "Girl tries to walk away to avoid getting hurt" part of the story. However, as we all know so well, change doesn't happen overnight and every girl has her kryptonite. In this case, it was "Boy spills his heart out and makes it seem like maybe, there was hope after all," and I told you exactly where that landed me.

As you can see, even though I was able to deal with my issues during my man-fast, I couldn't heal and completely be whole until I was able to shake that one last situation. Consequently, this time, things ended differently. Although this situation hurt me far more than any of the others, I didn't walk away with more baggage. Yes, I walked away with my feelings completely shattered, but this time I handled it a little differently. I didn't stick around the situation so that my feelings could continue to be misused, abused and dragged through the mud. I didn't hold my tongue to prevent showing any signs of vulnerability. I didn't feel like I could never trust again. I didn't call him names, curse him out or try to make him feel my wrath. Instead, I gracefully walked away with my dignity and a brand new mindset. I looked to one of my favorite Bible verses for comfort, Psalm 84:11, which says "...The Lord bestows favor and honor; no good thing does he withhold from those who walk uprightly." It reassured me that God had something much better planned.

I truly believe that the difference between this time and the previous times was the fact that I had taken that moment to pause and begin to teach myself how to treat *me*. We're so quick to defend our little sisters, cousins, and best friends against others, yet we let people treat us any old kind of way in the name of love. Since I now recognized the patterns and methods I used when dealing with situations in the past, I was able to change the way I looked at this circumstance. Although I was hurt, I spent my time trying to learn how to forgive, rather than jumping into the arms of someone else during an emotionally unstable time. I took time to reflect, alone, and let God show me what He needed to reveal.

The next time a guy disappoints you, give yourself some time to cool off and heal. (By time, I don't mean just a few weeks either.) If you don't, you'll go into the next situation already somewhat predisposed to fail. Like an air mattress that's been jumped on, you're a bit deflated— whether it is mentally, emotionally, or even physically, until eventually there's no air left at all. You don't want to get to that place! You need to take care of your heart just like you would any other part of your body that is injured!

When it comes to heartache and pain, the crash is usually something we can see coming from a mile away. Think about the last guy that did you wrong. Can you honestly say that the signs were never there? Maybe some of us can say we were completely thrown for a loop, but more often than not, most of us saw it coming; we ignored the signs and then acted completely shocked when it all hit the fan. To be completely honest with myself, in retrospect, I can't say I've ever been completely surprised. The signs were always there, I just chose to ignore them. It happens to the best of us.

Your central nervous system produces the sensation of pain. It's a survival mechanism that your body uses to keep you alive. The sensation of pain must occur in order to alert the body that something is wrong. It draws attention to the source so that you will avoid a repeat occurrence. If we didn't feel pain, we'd never know something was wrong. We could break every bone in our bodies over and over again without even realizing it. When you experience the pain of heartache, realize that the same survival mechanism is occurring. Realize that as bad as it may seem, when you are experiencing heartache, you may be BRUISED, but you are not BROKEN. When someone is bruised, they feel physical or emotional pain in their body, but they are not physically incapable of completing the task at hand. You hit your funny bone on a table and you feel a great sensation of pain, but you can keep on moving because you know that the feeling will not last long. It may be uncomfortable, but you know that you just have to shake it off and go on about your business. When you are injured and break a bone, you are physically incapable of moving forward. You are crippled and must seek help and medical attention. Whether it is an actual broken bone, or just something that is no longer working as it should, you are physically handicapped.

A few things to remember when you feel heartache from a failed relationship: Your heart is not physically broken! You are just in pain, and in time, the pain will become manageable and even, some day, may not even cause you any more sadness. Just because someone let you down does not mean you are now crippled, handicapped, or in need of an EMS truck. It's okay to cry it out, but don't allow yourself to feel as though you will never love or be loved again. If it could be taken from you, chances are it wasn't for you in the first place. If your situation is bringing out the worst in you, or stunting your growth and progression, chances are you may need to cut ties. I know he was such a great guy at first and you're not really sure where and why things started to go wrong. I feel your pain honey, but the fact of the matter is, you have to pick yourself up and look at things for what they are. I know it hurts. A lot. However, please understand that your heart is not broken in half, it's just a little bruised and in need of some rest and relaxation. Sometimes it's hard to snap out of the sad, lonely daze you feel when someone has "broken your heart." I've realized that there's really no cure for that but God, time, forgiveness, and responsibility. The cure to getting over someone is NOT getting under someone else, despite what the world has tricked you into believing.

Let yourself out of the prison called unforgiveness, the one where you constantly torture yourself with the memory of how much someone hurt you. Unforgiveness in your heart keeps you stagnant and stuck in the past. So why voluntarily enslave yourself to circumstances or people? You have to let it all go in order to move on and be able to accept the next phase of your life. Give yourself time to heal, but acknowledge what role you played in the situation. Realize what you accepted and where you could have demanded to be treated differently. Most importantly, you have to move on, not only with your words—by saying you're over it—but with your actions. If you can't see a post he makes on Instagram, see him out in public, or hear his name without getting upset or causing a scene, chances are, you really aren't over it yet. You also must be willing to move on, even if it means doing so before you receive an apology, if ever, from him. Real forgiveness doesn't depend on the other person, it's all for your personal growth and peace of mind.

My pastor, Dr. Jermone T. Glenn (Revolution Christian Ministries) once said these words that have forever stuck with me, "Just because I am attracted to you does not mean I am assigned to you or you are assigned to me. If you try to make an attraction your assignment you will be frustrated over and over again because attraction does not equal assignment." Basically, every man that you like is not your husband. Remember that. Just because he's your boyfriend right now, doesn't mean he's supposed to be your husband later. Let that sink in. God has designed someone specifically for you. Once you grasp and trust that fact, life and the ability to "let go" becomes a whole lot easier.

Looking back on it all now, I see why I had to learn those lessons back then. Now, at this point in my life, I can't afford to find myself in any emotionally draining situations again. My career, my purpose and my future are all at stake. Although none of those situations ended the way I may have initially hoped, I wouldn't trade the experience for anything. The lessons I learned have ultimately made me a better person. Therefore, I cannot be mad. I cannot be bitter. Thanks to those experiences, I was forced to learn lessons of forgiveness. I was also able to identify what characteristics I desire, as well as what I will not accept in my future husband. Most importantly, I learned a lot about myself. About my flaws, and what personal insecurities I needed to address for my own good.

Personal insecurities will have you ruining a friendship or relationship quicker than anything else. I realized that instead of trying to be the "perfect girl" all the time, a chameleon adapting to what I thought someone would like or appreciate, I just needed to be myself. I realized that I don't have to play the "tough girl" role, denying my feelings or preventing myself from opening up. I see now that instead of pretending to be indifferent about the pace a relationship is moving, or the lack of "titles" in a situationship, it is better to be honest with myself as well as the other person. My tendency to avoid commitment was rooted in my fear of abandonment. A fear that existed only because I wasn't yet confident in who I am and what all I could bring to the table in a relationship.

I am so grateful that I was able to come to understand how relationships, or should I say, the wrong relationships could block me from my destiny. I thought I was superwoman and could multitask it all. It wasn't until I was able to rid myself of certain distractions that I could clearly see what else I could be doing with my time, like building my relationship with the Lord, and walking in my purpose. It wasn't until I truly let go of the pain from my relationships/situationships and began to embrace my singlehood, that I was able to accept and embrace my life for what it was. It wasn't until then that I understood that God will one day reveal the special guy he has just for me, when the time is right. The same goes for you!

Appreciate how truly valuable you are....
And act accordingly.

"I am beautiful. No matter what they say.
Words can't bring me down.
I am beautiful, in every single way.
Yes, words can't bring me down. Oh no." - ***Christina Aguilera***

If you don't know who you are, you won't know what you need. If you don't know what you need, you won't know what you don't need. When you don't know what you don't need, you'll tolerate anything. Once you tolerate anything, you'll lose everything. If that last chapter made you feel a little uncomfortable, or had you thinking about a few relationships or situationships in your past or maybe even present, then I suggest you refer back to the advice given in chapter one and perform a mirror check on yourself! Start analyzing so you can start fixing! Your might be asking yourself, “How do I do this?” Well, first you have to admit that you want better for yourself. Like I said in chapter one, what works best for me is writing my feelings down. Sometimes it helps to vent or discuss with someone you love and trust. Whatever you do, you have to talk/write/sort through your feelings, emotions, and habits so that you can recognize they exist in the first place. It’s hard to fix faulty patterns when you’re in denial. Sometimes, you have to go and talk to that one person you know won’t sugar coat the truth for you. Talk to the person that you haven’t asked for advice yet, because you’re afraid of the bold truth they’ll give you. Chances are, that is just the advice you need to give you the boost to move forward. You have to fix that broken pattern, so that you will be able to receive the GREAT man of God that the Lord has for you when the time comes. You can’t accept him, flaws and all, until you can get yourself together. The problem starts and stops with YOU. Believe it or not, people, especially men, are watching how you carry yourself, how you react to situations, and how you treat yourself in order to decide what level of respect they think they owe you.

Why do we allow people to treat us with less respect than we deserve? Why do we sacrifice our dignity for other’s gain or approval? The only answer that makes sense to me is that we aren't aware of our self-worth. Think about it, when was the last time you saw someone throw a "$1" bill into one of those water fountains at the mall? Probably never. But how many pennies, nickels and dimes are lying at the bottom of that pool? From the outside looking in, a penny, nickel, and dime seem to be made of material that is much stronger, more durable and of greater value than that of a paper dollar. Yet, we have enough sense to protect flimsy paper dollars in our wallets, safe and sound, while we drop loose change on the ground, in the cup holders of our cars, or in those mall fountains. Are you not worth more than a paper dollar? Why do you conduct your life in such a manner that you allow yourself to be treated like chump change? You let people drop you when they feel like it, store you in the back of their mind or priorities, then pick you back up when it's convenient for them.

One of my close male friends once explained to me why he believes many men treat women the way they do. He said that the reason men treat women with such little respect, is because they know that with the bare minimum amount of effort, they'll still get what they want from a majority of women. Sounds simple enough right? It's an age-old tale, you know, "*Why settle for the cow when you can get the milk for free.*" Good thing you're not giving away your milk for free right. Wrong. It's deeper than the physical, and goes way beyond sex. Our generation is slowly killing the concept that once was chivalry. Unlike the famous Instagram quote, I don't believe "chivalry died when women started calling it [thirst]." This quote suggests that men stopped behaving in a chivalrous manner because women were unappreciative and mocked this behavior, suggesting the man is desperate. I find this to be false. A *true* gentlemen's conduct should not be contingent upon reciprocation. If you ask me, chivalry began to die when the idea of being ladies and gentlemen became a thing of the past. When people began to glorify the behavior of pimps, players, strippers, home wreckers, and half-naked celebrities in the media, they made such behavior *the norm,* a more celebrated concept than behaving upright and modest. We need more role models so that our young people grow up knowing how to treat one another, as well as how they deserve to be treated.

Our lack of respect for ourselves, for one another, and a blatant dismissal of loyalty has made it hard for chivalry to exist. Little boys don't know what it means to be a man, or how women should be treated. Little girls don't even realize how much respect they should expect.

I've heard guys say that women often underestimate how much power they really have. We have the ability to set the tone. When women think its funny and perfectly fine to be a "sidechick" we are becoming a part of the problem. When women claim to have high standards, yet abandon them to get a guy's attention, what message does that send? Where's the mystery? Where is the challenge? It doesn't exist in most cases. After a week or two of consistent "Good morning" texts half of us are ready to marry the guy. All he really had to do was twiddle his thumbs, literally, and now you like him... because of some text messages. Half the time he probably didn't even have to actually pick up the phone and call you before you're telling your home-girls about your new "BAE." You didn't make him take you on a date. And by date, I mean a real date. Where he picks you up, opens the door, takes you to the destinations, **PAYS,** and brings you back home safely, unharmed and untouched. Nope, he didn't have to really do a thing. You're content with weeks, maybe even months of....text messages. You know, messages of what "will be..." one day, or never. Either way, it's not today. That was cool in middle school, but honey, we're grown now! Don't get me wrong, I'm not judging you, I've been there too! I'm not trying to be harsh, but I wish someone had been blunt with me like this! I never thought I was that girl until it was too late. I guess it's just something about "heart eye" emoji's from our crushes that'll really activate the butterflies in our stomachs, and the stupidity in our brains. So let's just make a promise to ourselves right here and now, and that's to remember that actions speak louder than text messages.

That eye-opening epiphany led me to see just how much the flow of the dating process really begins with a woman respecting herself. Women have become so accustomed to the idea that men won't put in work anymore and that chivalry is dead, that they have indeed eliminated many requirements and standards in dating. If a man knows that he can put in twenty-five percent of his effort to get a girl to give him the time of day, then he's going to do just that. Nothing more, nothing less. Men don't go above and beyond anymore because you don't make them! Imagine if more women put their foot down and raised their standards.... men would have no choice but to step up! However, they won't have any reason to step up, until women do.

I believe the hardest part in operating according to your worth is 1) knowing how to create standards and stick to them and 2) learning to conquer loneliness.

As women, we are natural-born caregivers. After all, we were created for such. Many of us are very nurturing and tend to see the good in our partners. We see the potential we believe they have to be the greatest boyfriend, friend, husband, or father. Without the right amount of self-confidence, this can go either way. On the one hand, without enough self-confidence, or without realizing her worth, a woman will stick around in a relationship that isn't healthy or positive. On the other hand, she may be too insecure to truly believe that her man is being faithful to her and only her. Ladies, there are some GREAT men in this world. Plenty of dogs, but nonetheless, lots and lots of decent guys! However, based on my observations of men, I've come to one conclusion: Men know exactly how to act, when they want to. The problem is, it just may not be with you.

A woman will invest so much time, months and years, waiting for her man to get it right or "learn how to act." In reality, more often than not, if a man wants to keep you and truly believes that you are the only woman for him, he will do whatever it is in his power to keep you in his life. That includes making sacrifices and putting his woman's happiness first. At the same time, a lot of men don't like being alone, so they'll also do what they have to do to keep a girl around for convenience, not necessarily for keeps. So many women are so desperate for love that they'll settle for being someone's convenient option, rather than waiting to be someone else's one and only choice.

Nobody should settle for being one of someone's options, a member of someone's "team." However, you have to know and believe that about yourself before you can expect someone else to believe it. If you tell a man you're not looking for a relationship, you can't expect him to think of you, or treat you like girlfriend material. When you tell a man that from the beginning, you are ultimately setting a low standard, despite the fact that you probably only said it to avoid sounding too desperate or clingy. Don't get it twisted though, I'm not saying just jump right into it like, "Hey, I'm trying to be your next girlfriend." It's definitely important to let things flow naturally and really get to know a person. I'm just saying, when you're cooking his dinner every night, washing his clothes, buying him gifts, and giving up the cookie, after you told him you're cool with just being friends, who are you trying to fool? Him or yourself? Set the standard and leave it up to him to meet you there. If he does, you may be on to something. If he doesn't, well then now you know. My point is, we leave a lot of room for gray area in how we claim we want to be treated, when we don't even set the tone in the first place.

One thing I commend a lot of men on is the fact that many of them know exactly what they want, when they want it, and don't settle for anything less. Notice I said *many*, not all. It's rare that you see a man mistakenly "falling into love." Usually they've made a decision that 1) this woman is someone they can envision themselves with long term, 2) someone they can trust, and 3) let it be known that they're ready to give up the games and "other women." They know how to separate the "fun" from the "serious relationships" and how to realistically position themselves so they can be a provider in order to be a great partner. Women, we're just all over the place. One minute we're just going on a date with "a friend" who we couldn't see much of a future with and the next minute we're all in love "with his personality" and his "bright future." How many times have you ended up in a relationship, or probably a situationship, with someone you had no intentions of being with in the first place? It has certainly happened to me! We get a taste of what we think we want and get caught up in our bliss. Men get a taste of what they want and then think, "Well, if I could get her, then I know I could get someone better." I'm not saying that's the best mentality to have, but it sure would be nice to be able to see clearly past the butterflies for once, wouldn't it?

Another tendency I've noticed is that we, as women, often confuse a man not knowing what he wants as far as a relationship is concerned, for a man simply just not wanting US. Women think with emotion. Men think with logic. Therefore, a woman will evaluate a situation in which a man isn't putting in as much effort anymore as him being scared of commitment, scared of rejection, or waiting on her to make the first move. This is where we begin to lose in the game of love.

While those options may be true in some cases, most often if a guy isn't putting in the effort, it's not because he isn't aware of how to treat you, but because simply put, *he just doesn't want to*. Simple as that. Ouch.

Why do you think so many guys go from being players and mistreating and misleading women, to finding one woman, falling in love and being a great boyfriend/husband? Let me assure you, he didn't suddenly enroll in a "How to be a Perfect Gentlemen" class. He simply found someone that made him realize that he needed to get his act together. He finally met his match, the one he will probably treat like a queen in order to keep her in his life. STOP TRYING TO BE EVERYONE'S QUEEN! It's just not possible and that's OKAY! It doesn't matter how great of a girl you are, how much you cook, clean, support, sleep with...whatever, to a man, if he doesn't want to commit to you wholeheartedly, then he won't.

Think about all the good guys you've probably turned down or ignored in your lifetime. You probably didn't do so because they weren't good people, but because they just weren't the one for you. That doesn't mean they couldn't be perfect for someone else, and I'm sure you wouldn't want them to second-guess their worth just because you personally didn't want to be with them. Just because a guy doesn't appreciate your value, or decides that he doesn't want to be with you, doesn't make you any less beautiful, special, or girlfriend/wife material. The moment we start to question ourselves because someone doesn't want us, is the moment we start knocking down our own stock value. I've seen plenty of guys turn down or "play" my nice, pretty, great friends, only to end up with a girl that seemed to only measure up to half of what my friend was!

We can sit and wonder all day long why he chose one girl over the other. You can speculate and come up with theory after theory of why he didn't want to be with you. Nonetheless, at the end of the day, his choice does not determine your worth. You just aren't the girl for him! Sometimes that doesn't even mean he thinks any less of you, it just means, you're not his "one."

But everything was going great. You two were vibing. What did you do wrong? You were the perfect girl, right? He even told you so... Well, that could be true! Sometimes men who aren't ready for the real deal will run from you, avoiding commitment, if you seem to be the type of girl that would require them to step up. In that case, they're doing you a favor. Sometimes they're too immature to even realize what they're doing and how good of a woman you are anyway.

The Bible says in Matthew 7:6, "Do not give dogs what is sacred; do not throw your pearls to pigs. If you do, they may trample them under their feet, and turn and tear you to pieces." You wouldn't give a dog your favorite shoe to play with and you certainly wouldn't give a pig your favorite pearl necklace, because you know they don't have the knowledge and wisdom to appreciate such valuables. Just because a pig will trample pearls under its feet, doesn't mean that the pearls are now worth the same as the rocks and dirt they're lying in. It just means that the pig has no idea what he's dealing with.

When someone doesn't see your value, it may be because they don't have the eyes to even focus on what they're seeing. The pearls are still pearls even if a pig can't comprehend that fact. It's up to you to remember your self-worth, even when dogs and pigs don't.

Now on to my next point: Loneliness. It is often time extremely hard for people to exhibit patience when it comes to dating. I think we've have become so accustomed to entertaining the wrong guy while waiting on the right guy, because we do not know how to be ALONE. I mean, it's not always that we really *believe* in our heart of hearts that Mr. Wrong is Mr. Right—he's actually more like Mr. Keep Me Company, but nonetheless—we're just giving him more of ourselves than we should. It's honestly pretty sad when you think about it. Think about how many times you've settled for something you know for a fact is temporary, just to "keep yourself busy." Most of us have done it, that's for sure. The problem with that is, no matter how much you think you're just "casually dating", feelings still eventually bloom. Then like I said earlier, somewhere down the line it's like you forget that they weren't supposed to be around for the long run anyway. So why do we do that? At 21, 22, 23, 24, 25 and up why in the world are we still acting like we did in high school, dating guys we'd never truly want to marry, have children with, and live happily ever after with? We'll basically just waste time, energy, emotion, and years of our lives on guys we really don't see a future with all because we do not know how to be content in our singlehood. And, by single I mean unmarried. Just because he's playing house with you, doesn't mean you've "won."

There are certain lessons we as women (and men too) are supposed to learn, accomplish, and experience prior to becoming someone's spouse. It is often times extremely difficult to learn those lessons while involved with someone. It's certainly not impossible to grow with another person, as a matter of fact, it's quite common that a relationship is just want a person needs to move to the next level in their life. However, more often than not, when you are in a relationship your focus is on how to make "US" work, how can "WE" grow together, what can "YOU" do for me and what can I do for you. That's all fine and dandy, but when do we focus on OURSELVES? When do we have the freedom enough to be completely selfish, focusing on our own needs and wants, figuring out what makes us happy, and what exactly we want in a partner? Many would probably argue that being single has nothing to do with that self-growth process, but I'd have to disagree. At least for my personal life. The moment I decided to take a break from my dating cycle and get myself together is when my life began to take off! It wasn't until I removed myself from certain situations/people that I even realized what was going on! It wasn't that I hadn't previously cared about my future or wasn't concerned with becoming the best me I could be. It's just that my focus was off. At the end of the day instead of plotting my next move, reflecting on what mattered most, or working on my relationship with God, I was on the phone, on Face Time or cuddled up. My life needed balance. Direction, if you will. But who really wants to think about life, the future, and grown up decisions when there's someone waiting to cake, as my generation calls it, with you at night?

As I grew in my relationship with God, I began to listen to my instincts more. They were telling me that I needed to consciously take myself out the dating game. So, for an entire year I didn't entertain any new prospects. Instead, I took a look in the mirror and faced everything I needed to deal with...and boy was that liberating.

I was sick of finding myself in the same situation time after time. I was tired of getting excited about a new possibility, only to be disappointed. I was more sick and more tired of lowering and bending my standards all to keep losing in the end anyway. The man fast was a good step, but I felt I needed to take it a step forward. So, I did like Michael Jordan and took a break. Like I said in the beginning, this isn't a book of hardcore step-by-step advice. It's just my story. Maybe everyone doesn't need a hiatus, but I did. I couldn't think straight while still entertaining the thought of a boyfriend. I reevaluated what was most important to me, which realigned my focus, thus eliminating my distractions and opening up space and opportunity for me to thrive.

After my yearlong man-vacation, I started to get back out there in the dating scene. However, it was like suddenly I'd become too smart for my own good. The rose-colored glasses I'd once worn had been removed, and I now had the innate ability to see things for what they really were. Meaning, I was totally allergic to the bull crap.

You see, there's something about conquering the feeling of LONELINESS that allows you to make significantly smarter decisions, and see things much more clearly than you could when you were single, thirsty and on the prowl. It's like we want a drink so bad that whatever they're offering, *provided it's decent,* we're down to drink it because it quenches our thirst. Think about a super-hot day when sweat is dripping down your face and your mouth is as dry as ever. You probably think to yourself, "Man a cold glass of fresh, homemade lemonade would hit the spot right now." If in that next moment, your friend offered you a cold can of not so homemade, not so fresh, maybe even a little tart, lemonade, chances are you wouldn't turn it down. You'd drink it, because you'd tell yourself that in that moment, any lemonade would do the trick. In a nutshell, that's what I had been doing all those years. As long it kind of looked or sounded like a relationship, I was going to try to make it work.

Now let's take that same scenario and flip it. On a not so hot day, you're sitting in a comfortable air-conditioned restaurant and you order freshly squeezed lemonade from your waitress. You sip on the complimentary water she brought you as you wait patiently for your drink. She comes out and brings you a can of off brand lemonade and a cup of ice. You've had this brand of lemonade before, so you already know it's not that sweet, and usually leaves a bad aftertaste. Because you're not dying of thirst, you are a bit pickier, and have a lot more patience to wait on what you really want. So, you tell the waitress you'll continue to drink your water and wait until she can bring you the correct drink.

When I became content with it being God and I in my picture, I suddenly gained a never-ending supply of everything I ever needed. My cup became so full with His love that I didn't NEED it to be filled by anything or anyone else. I had no desire to seriously entertain someone I didn't see myself with for the sole purpose of just having someone around. Due to the fact that I had learned to be fine with being by my lonesome, my "thirst" was redirected to what mattered most. I was thirsty for God; thirsty to live out to my full potential; thirsty to see the maximum outcome birthed out of my life. You can fake it all you want, but until you truly are okay with being alone, you won't understand how I was able to 1) be happily alone for over a year 2) come out of it and not want to jump right into the very thing I'd desired so much (love). It wasn't that I had a heart of stone or became emotionless. In fact, I was probably even more in touch with my emotions than ever before at this point. However, I had come to a point in my life where I wasn't seeking anything but God and how to live out my purpose. I was fulfilled. So, anything a random guy could bring to the table would just be dessert, not the main course...and as tasty as it may be, I could live without a cookie.

"Knowing your worth and God's very thoughts, love and promises for YOUR life will keep you from lending your mind to certain conversations and people" are wise words spoken by my dear friend, Marchelle Miles. Until you spend time getting to know the word of God and learning to hear His voice, it may be almost impossible to truly know your worth.

The Bible is filled with proclamations and promises of how special each and every one of God's children are to Him. When you strengthen your walk with Him, He will show you who you really are. That is exactly why it is so hard for a true believer, and someone who is actively trying to walk with Christ, to submit to the wicked ways of this world, no matter how popular they may be. It becomes harder and very awkward to knowingly downgrade yourself for people who don't even value their own lives, let alone yours.

If one day, designer Christian Louboutin let someone convince him that he should let his classic red bottom shoes be sold in dollar stores because more people could afford them and he'd get more customers, think about what would happen to his brand? It would be worthless within a matter of days, hours even. People appreciate his brand because it is of high quality. Not everyone can get it, and he knows it! He doesn't feel the need to downgrade his prices and availability for the sake of gaining more customers because he values the worth of his product. Are you downgrading your standards and morals for the sake of more attention? Are you afraid that if you decide not to sleep with him, or decide to set up boundaries in your dating life, that you won't get any attention because your price is too high? Well ponder on this quote I once heard from Marshawn Evans, "A diamond doesn't step down just because cubic zirconia's are getting more attention."

You keep lowering your standards and you'll keep getting a lower caliber of men! I know they say good girls finish last, but wouldn't you rather finish last with his last name, than first with a throwaway consolation prize of memories and heartache? Look at dating as one of those dance marathon competitions rather than a rat race. It's not about who can get a boyfriend or a husband the quickest. It's about who can stay out there and stand their ground until the time comes to claim your prize, or should I say until your prize claims you. The word of God says, "he that findeth a wife, findeth a good thing" (Proverbs 18:22).

With all of that being said, I strongly encourage YOU to take some quiet time to yourself, embark on some type of fast or personal recovery journey. I can't really tell you what to do or how to do it. Only YOU know what it is that's controlling your mind, thoughts, and emotions. Gain control of the silent chaos that exists in your world, or even just in your mind. I promise you it will change your whole life, just take a quick look inside of you. Once nobody else is there, you're stuck alone staring in the mirror. Those thoughts you've been shoving under the rug for months, or years, are then slapping you right in the face. Once that happens, and once you deal with whatever it is accordingly, I guarantee you will be able to begin to pull it together. You are meant to be great! It's up to you to clear away the clutter so that your light can shine.

Everyone always laughs at the scene in the movie, "The Help," when Abilene told young Mae, "You Is Kind. You Is Smart. You Is Important." If you saw the movie, then you know how impactful those words were. You are created in the image of God. He created you to be exactly how He wanted and needed you to be. Wishing you were someone else, or lived someone else's life is like criticizing God on the great job He did designing you.

There is nothing wrong with drawing inspiration from other people and what they've accomplished. Just make sure you're striving to be the best YOU that you can be, not to be a carbon copy of someone else. When I say strive to be the best you, I mean don't dumb yourself down or hold back for fear of being judged. Don't worry about being different, or how you'll be received. Don't even worry about who will stick around and who will walk away. As long as you're being true to yourself, nothing else matters. Guess what? While you're so busy feeling self-conscious and shy about embracing who you really are, the very people you're hiding from are out there being themselves and could not care any less what you think about it!

Epiphany 4

'Seek Ye First the Kingdom of God,
and his righteousness, and all these
things shall be added unto you.'
Matthew 6:33

"I'm calling on you heavenly Father
I'm down on my knees.
You said call on you no matter the hour,
...Lord I'm in need." - **Isaac Carree**

Remember back in chapter one when I told you that once you spend honest tangible time getting to know God, He will in turn show you, you! Well, that's what we're going to think about next. Some of the questions I've had are: How do I spend time with someone I can't see? How do I listen to God? How exactly can He speak to me?

I didn't understand this at first, but boy am I learning more and more about it every single day. Here's what I've realized thus far, so I want to pass it along to you. Like I said, I'm still learning myself, but hopefully it'll be of some help to you.

You have to establish a prayer life. You have to spend alone time in solitude to express your desires, concerns, and everything else to Him. You should take the time to just thank Him for everything that He is! He WILL communicate with you. God isn't some big golden statue that you pray to, only to get no response. He speaks to me through other people. Sometimes I'll pray for something, and not too long after someone will contact me and say something that confirms what I just prayed about. Or I'll hear something at church, on the radio, or on TV that encourages or reassures me. Sometimes I'll just be thinking about something, and all of a sudden an encouraging idea, thought, or scripture will come to me that I was absolutely not in the mental capacity or state to come up with myself.

Other times it's just a feeling. For example, I'll consider one option and feel totally uneasy about it, but then I'll consider another and suddenly be completely at peace. Instinct.

What's really interesting is when I'm having a mental conversation with myself, and I'll feel like a voice is interrupting my thoughts as if someone is actually talking back to me. Sometimes it's my own voice, sometimes it's the voice of someone else; such as me remembering something my parents or pastor once said. This little voice will play like a recording in a moment when I'm not consciously trying to think positively either. Sometimes it'll happen in a moment when I'm trying to sulk, and the last thing I want to hear is something profound. Many may call it your conscience. I call it the Holy Spirit!

At times I know God has spoken to me through my disappointments. It's like He's upgraded my wants and desires by allowing things I once wanted to fail. When things start to fail you start to reevaluate and consider other options. You seek wise counsel and other people's opinions. You become humble enough to realize that maybe your way isn't working, especially when they fail over and over and over again.

Hearing from God may be different for everyone. Pastor Glenn told us, "God will get into what you're into." So, basically that means He will speak to you in the way that is most effective for you personally. A relationship with God is a real relationship. So, no, if you've been waiting for a "Lion King" like experience where Simba's reflection began to talk back to him in the pond, and then the skies opened up and Mufasa's face appeared in the clouds as James Earl Jones' deep voice echoed loud and clear for Simba to hear, then I can see why you'd be confused. Sure God CAN do that. He can do anything. And He will! Isaiah 19:1, Revelation 1:7, and Deuteronomy 33:26 all tell us that He will most definitely come riding through the clouds for the entire world to see. However, as far as your everyday life, you've got to dig a little deeper and learn to hear the silent whispers of God that are actually more LOUD and clear than we realize! John 10:27 says, "My sheep listen to my voice; I know them, and they follow me."

Listen to His voice, trust His voice, and move according to His voice.

Even the least spiritual person will call on God in a moment of crisis. Why is it that we expect such supernatural blessings from God, but won't even give Him the minimum earthly time and commitment we give to other things? We commit to give every Sunday to him as if that's something to brag over. Can you imagine what your boyfriend/girlfriend, mother, best friend would say if you told them well, I talked to you on Sunday, so be happy. No! When you love someone you go above and beyond to make him or her happy. Not because you want something back or because it's expected, you do it because you want to. God wants you above all. He wants you to acknowledge Him for all He is in your life, so that you can be a light that others are drawn to.

When you're living the righteous life, people are drawn to you because they can see that there's something about you that seems so fulfilling. Something that they lack. Perhaps it's your peace that passes all understanding. Or, maybe it could be from your unwavering, unfaltering joy, and the joy that comes from The Lord being your strength. Not saying you're always perky and jolly, always in a great mood, and not human, but there is such a joy that even on the worst days, when everything may seem to be crumbling around you, you have a peace, a security, all because of your love and personal relationship with Jesus Christ. People will wonder how you can still praise God in the midst of a storm, and why is it that you are so confident in your future when your present shows little to no signs of success. That is how you are a light in the darkness. Everyone won't understand your praise, but any curious mind will want to inquire as to why things always seem to work out for you, and why you don't seem to be as depressed, lonely, and hurt as them.

People are always so quick to stuff a bible down someone's throat, judge them, tell them that everything they're doing wrong is sending them straight to hell, and then wonder why nobody wants to come to church. You can't always scare someone out of going to hell. Maybe you could if an eternal life of pain and suffering didn't sound all too familiar to their current life. Now I'm not one for sugar coating, I believe that it is up to us to share the absolute truth of the gospel with the world. However, God is the judge, not us. We as believers have to live such a life that people feel pressed to know the God we serve. When someone loses a lot of weight, others who are seeking those same results begin to pay attention. They want to know what strategies that person used, what foods they ate, what workout regimen they implemented to get to their current status. They aren't inquiring because they want that person to scream and tell them they are fat, undisciplined, lazy, and unwelcome in their private gym club. In the event that was how they were addressed, while some may respond positively, most will retreat and back away, embarrassed, looking for another way to escape from their misery. I believe the same goes with bringing others to Christ. Granted, every relationship and experience is different. Some people will be responsive; however, many people, especially those that don't know you well enough to ensure you have their best interest at hand, will feel judged. If someone is coming to you for advice regarding the subject in the first place, they probably already know deep down that the life they are living is not right. They don't always need you to reprimand them for that. It is the Holy Spirit's job to convict their spirit. Sure the Holy Spirit may even speak through you, giving you words that convict, but nonetheless it is not you, it is Him who does so. Your job is to be an example, a walking billboard that leads them to God, who is more than capable to handle it from there.

As I learn how to become a better Christian, and representative of the Kingdom of God, I've put away many things. Things that used to bother me no longer concern me. I even find myself not responding to drama and negativity the way I used to because I'm now in a much better, more solemn place. You can't hide from whom you really are inside, because eventually your innermost thoughts and emotions are displayed in your actions. Make sure that you're working on what's going on in that head of yours. Give it up to God and realize that you don't always have to have the last word. You don't always have to get them back, or prove them wrong. Vengeance is the Lord's.

To move forward and strengthen your relationship with the Lord, you absolutely need like-minded people around you. I truly believe God gave me such friends as the crew I have so that we could grow together and actually witness what a Godly friendship between normal, growing people looks like. Not just what it should look like. Not what it looks like between people on a movie, or people in church, or the public eye. We see that it is possible for God to infiltrate all areas of your life to such a degree that He makes His way into a majority of your conversations, not to brag or sound good or impress, but because he's a part of YOU. To be able to express your thoughts, desires, fears, and battles against spiritual warfare with friends without having to dumb it down, or be afraid of sounding crazy or too holy because they understand and are going through the same things is priceless.

I believe many people get to this place where they want to grow in their relationship with God, but since an environment where such a lifestyle is understood or appreciated doesn't surround them, they retreat and fall back. When you see your best friends growing in Christ, it should only make you want to grow as well! When your best friends are going on a 30-day man fast with you, or getting up at 6 a.m. for a prayer challenge with you, it can only strengthen your beliefs and willingness to fight the good fight because you are holding each other accountable. When you have a listening ear to give you wise counsel regarding what's going on in your world, what sins you're battling, or what giants you're trying to slay you'll probably make better choices. If nobody around you understands the narrow path you're attempting to walk, then it may be hard to convince yourself that what you're doing is ultimately best for you. Get around some like- minded people!

I thank GOD for my friendships because they taught me about relationships and showed me real genuine care, loyalty, and support. Besides all that I learned from my family, my friendships taught me the foundation of positive human relationships, which is God and friendship. We look out for each other because we became FAMILY. Nobody could come in and tear us apart. We're going to support each other as we walk through life as strong Kingdom citizens.

The point I'm trying to make here, is that when you put God first in your life, everything else will fall into place. When you are a born again believer, with Christ at the center of your life, you have the Holy Spirit there to guide you through every single day of your life. Read your bible, find a home church with a good pastor, and take the time to get to know Him! You need a peaceful center at the core of your life in this crazy world.

Epiphany 5

Life WILL throw you lemons...
the lemonade is made when you
consciously decide to grow
through your hard times.

"I'm a survivor.
I'm not gon' give up.
I'm not gon' stop.
I'm gon' work harder.
I'm a survivor, I'm gonna make it.
I will survive, and keep on surviving." – **Destiny's Child**

The Struggle. It's something we all can relate to. You know the, "every time I take one step forward, I get knocked two steps back," or the "I just can't win" feeling. It sucks. Nobody really wants to struggle. Most people don't really embrace the struggle either. Yet for some odd reason, once we "make it," the struggle is the first thing we thank. We're quick to attribute our "started from the bottom" life experiences as one of the major contributors to our success story. Drake said it best.

Why is that? Well, when it's all said and done, we're mature enough to know that "what doesn't kill us makes us stronger," that "it takes a test to produce a testimony," and that "nothing worth having comes easily." We know that! In retrospect at least. We live by it. We have it plastered on our walls, and tattooed on our bodies, yet as soon as the going gets tough, we forget all of that, and suddenly it's "woe is me." Some of you may even be going through hard times right now; feeling as if "your life is on the ground," as my good friend Christine always says. If that's you, moping around, basking in a pity party, letting your current struggle get the best of you all because you're unable to see past "right now," then this chapter is most definitely for you.

Truth be told, I almost didn't graduate from college. I mean, I literally wasn't sure if I was graduating until two days before my graduation ceremony. I was a biomedical science major and my worst enemies, Microbiology and Biochemistry were literally out to get me. Talk about a humbling experience. You see, all my life I was an extraordinary student. I was student of the month every year in elementary, always on the honor roll all through high school, and graduated with honors in the top 9th percentile of my senior class. School always came naturally to me. That was, until I got to college and chose to take pre-med classes. It wasn't too bad the first few years of college as I still managed to pull mostly A's and B's. However, those eventually fell to C's, C-'s and even a D or two as I got closer and closer to senior year. Once I was hit with Physics and Organic Chemistry things definitely shifted completely for the worse. As much as I studied, the results didn't seem to reflect my effort. I struggled all the way through my upperclassman years, quite similarly to a lot of my fellow classmates, struggling through a major that had us constantly questioning our intelligence. I wasn't accustomed to struggling this hard in science or school period.

My advisor suggested I pick a different major, something I would be *better* at. "After all, you have straight A's in all your non-science classes. You should consider a different career" is what I remember her telling me. Although she probably didn't mean it in a negative way, I took her suggestion as a huge slap in the face. It felt like she was telling me to give up, that I wasn't smart enough to complete my major, and would be better off doing something else. At that point, it became an issue of pride. I worked MY BUTT OFF to get through the rigorous curriculum; studying harder and longer hours than anyone I knew. There were some weekends where I'd literally wake up at 7am and study straight through to well past midnight, while everyone else was out enjoying themselves. What made it worse was that at the end of the semester, those that had been out partying all year were quick to get on social media and post screenshots of their 3.999 GPA's, while I sat at home in tears looking at my GPA that was stuck in the mid 2-point range. I didn't get it, and it just didn't feel fair. I worked so hard. I put my best foot forward, all for what seemed like nothing. However, in my mind, I was now way too far to even think about starting over with a new major. I just had to push through.

I'll never forget the day I walked out of my Microbiology final in the summer of 2012. That hopeless feeling that settled deep in my stomach, from knowing I had just ruined everything I'd been working so hard for. Up until that day, I was all set to graduate that coming December provided I passed all of my classes. I didn't even have to wait until grades were posted to know that I had just blown every chance I had of making that happen. It was over, all because of ONE class. My schedule for what was supposed to be my next and last semester of college was filled to capacity, and I had no room to makeup a failed class. I was devastated. After all, I'd studied for weeks and weeks and when I went to take the final exam, it all looked like Chinese to me. This had become an all too familiar feeling, and quite frankly, I really started to give up on myself, academically speaking. It was a terrible feeling. Had it not been for positive, caring people around me, like my parents who understood and comforted me rather than scolded me for pushing my graduation back an additional semester, I'm not sure what my next move would have been. They encouraged me to put my faith in God, and trust that He will provide a way. So, I wiped my tears and kept pushing, but barely. I came to grips with the fact that graduation for me would just have to happen in April of 2013. A date that at the time, felt so very far away.

So in that next semester, which was Fall 2012, life got real, and this time I failed Biochemistry. How in the world did I make it through my entire collegiate career without failing a class, and now when it really mattered, I couldn't seem to pass to save my life? Mind you, don't forget, I'm the girl who got straight A's most of her life, so to say I was feeling like a failure was an understatement. Since I failed Biochemistry, I had to retake it my last and final semester, along with Microbiology. My degree was pending upon two classes that had already DEFEATED me once. The pressure was definitely on. That last semester, hardly anyone saw me. I went ghost from a lot of my obligations. I quit my on-campus job and anything that I felt would take away potential study time. I became the most disciplined version of myself that I had ever seen. I went to every professor's office hour, every study session, and tutoring group I could find. I rode the bus 30 minutes downtown, to get on another bus further uptown—in a snowstorm—to sit in my professor's office for all of 15 minutes, multiple times a week if I needed to. I definitely started to see myself doing a little better on exams than I had the first time around, but I still wasn't passing with flying colors either. In all honesty, passing still didn't look all too promising. I needed a miracle.

Despite how many cards were stacked against me, I worked as hard as I could to prove to my parents, my professors and, most of all, myself that I deserved those passing grades. There were a lot of tears, a lot of headaches, and loads of frustration, but I kept the faith and God continued to carry me through. If you know anything about MY GOD, you know that He specializes in turning situations around in a way that only He can. He'll let you fall so close to rock bottom just so that you will give Him space and opportunity to show how miraculous he is. That's what you have to remember when you're going through something that seems extremely difficult and unattainable. As hard as it may be to you, it is never too hard for God, who is in you! Needless to say, even with all my hard work, my passing, and therefore graduation literally came down to my final exams...in both classes. Go figure right? If that wasn't stressful enough, what was more frightening was that I couldn't just barely pass my finals either. Nope, since they were worth a large percentage of my grade, it meant that I needed to get at least a C if I wanted to pass the class.

Seems simple enough right? Yeah, you'd think so, but with exams covering detailed information over roughly a 13-week period, a C can feel like an A+ sometimes. After five long years of studying all night, taking countless practice tests and writing dozens of papers.... a biochemistry exam and a microbiology exam stood between a degree and me.

I sacrificed sleep, food and almost my sanity those last few weeks of the semester. My sorority sister Diamond and I did EVERYTHING we could to try to pass those classes. Without her I couldn't have gotten through it. Most importantly, I called on God just about every second of the day. There was no way in the world I was going to allow two little tests to stop me from getting a degree, not after all the work I'd put into my education. Before I got to college, I never had to push myself mentally the way I had to those two years or so. Sure, I'd had to push myself in numerous other ways, but not with something that had previously come so naturally to me. It's humbling, and could have been very detrimental to my success and happiness, had I allowed it to be. I could've given up, said, "Forget it," and walked away. But that's when you have to take a step back and remember the bigger picture. Remember that God will never expect you to get through difficult situations alone. His grace is sufficient, and his power works best in our weakness. (2 Corinthians 12:9). He'd never give you a task to complete knowing you didn't stand a chance. I knew that I could do all things through Christ, and so that's exactly what I did. I think I ended up earning high B's on both of those exams if I remember correctly. Not only did God show up, He showed OUT.

On April 27, 2013, I walked across the stage with a Bachelor of Science degree in Biomedical Sciences from Grand Valley State University. A school ranked 7th of 45 four-year colleges and universities in the state of Michigan and 35th of over 150 universities in the Midwest Region that year.

I say this to reassure you that even when you feel like you're not going to make it, that your struggle is too big to conquer, with God on your side, and the right amount of drive, you WILL make it. You might not make it how you want to make it. You might not make it when you want to make it, but I promise you, God will see you through.

I admire Kobe Bryant. Not because he's the best since Michael Jordan, not because of the five championship rings, but because his character is undoubtedly praiseworthy. I know what it feels like to be the underdog, the one who's less likely to come out on top. Many of my classmates who were excelling in my major went to college preparatory high schools with rigorous curriculums that more than prepared them for the college course load. I did not. I started off already many steps behind everyone else. Now look at Kobe

Bryant back in 1996, the number 13 draft pick. Not number one, not number two or even three... 13. Who would've thought this guy would push his way to become one of the most relevant men in basketball history? He pushed through every obstacle and claimed victory until everyone else could see it too. At the end of the day, he didn't switch teams when the going got tough to look for a more comfortable situation. Instead, he worked hard to make his situation work and took on a leadership role to ensure his team would thrive. He has a desire to win like no other and puts his all into every single game as if it's down to the buzzer, and a ring is on the line. Just like Black Mamba, as he is known by his endearing fans, is how I want to be.

I know you all hear this time and time again, but I'm going to say it anyway. Sure it looks like everyone else around you is winning now, but if you remain steadfast and true, I guarantee you, your blessings will be so big that you'll be glad you didn't stick to the little plan you had before. Trust me, I'm a living example of that and since my story is probably not enough to convince you, let's take it to the bible. There are plenty examples in there of people who seemed to be LOSING when they were trying to do everything right, but they hung in there and God brought them out better than before.

Let's see, there's Joseph. A boy who was just trying to be a kid, following his father's orders and tending to his family's sheep. When you're doing what you're supposed to do, you're bound to have haters. Sometimes your own family! Little Joe was thrown into a pit and then sold into slavery by his own brothers. As if that wasn't enough, when he finally got out of that mess, he was thrown into jail for a crime he didn't commit. Like so many of us, he made friends with folks who ended up forgetting about him when they came up in the world. Well, eventually he was rewarded for his faithfulness. He ended up becoming the second in command in all of Egypt! Talk about a come-up.

Then there's Job. Job was a stand-up guy. He just wanted to live a Godly life and take care of his family. The devil was just like your typical hater. He tried to convince God that the only reason Job was so righteous was because he had never been through anything. God knew Job's heart, so he allowed some hardships to come Job's way to shut the devil up and prove him wrong. Job lost it all, his wife turned on him, his kids died, and all his animals and sources of wealth perished. He lost all of his power, his stamina, and his health began to fail. His friends told him God was out to get him and he should really just give up this whole "faith" thing. They even speculated that he must have done something terribly wrong to deserve all of this pain. Talk about fair-weather friends. But he didn't sin and turn against God. He persevered through the rough time. So, long story short, God ended up restoring to Job everything he lost, and then some. He gave him DOUBLE of all that he had in the first place. After that he was blessed with a long, happy life and lived to see his kids, grandkids, and great grandkids!

God will not let you struggle for no reason! If your victory doesn't seem to happen when you think it should, remember that God's timing is perfect because He is the author of time. He rewards those that are faithful, steadfast, and true. People are always watching you. Some are awaiting your downfall and others are counting on your success to be the very motivation they need to accomplish their own dreams and goals. They are watching to see how you handle conflict and hardships. You can either lead by a positive example, or lead them to destruction. Either way, there is a lesson in it all and it's up to you to make sure that your struggle isn't in vain.

Sometimes what we think is a struggle or a setback, is really God's covering and protection. One of the most difficult tasks in maturing in my relationship with Christ has been learning to accept the "no's." It's very hard, when I have my mind set on what I want, to stop and realize when God is telling me to slow down. Jeremiah 29:11 says, "For I know the plans I have for you says the Lord, plans to prosper you and not to harm you, plans to give you hope and a future." We must keep that verse in mind when something we had our hearts set on falls through. All that means is that it wasn't a part of God's plan. You never know whether things don't work out because God is protecting you from something or because He has something much greater in mind that you just can't see yet.

I can't count how many times I've been driving my car and have gotten extremely impatient after traveling behind a slow driver! I usually complain and try to make my way around the slow car, but sometimes I just get stuck in between a bunch of people driving at a turtle-like speed. On numerous occasions, in the middle of my road rage induced tongue lashing at the cars around me, I'll look out my window and realize that there is a police car sitting on the side of the road, just waiting to catch the next speeding vehicle that flies past. What a feeling of relief and gratitude that moment is, when I realize that I would have probably been speeding had that slow driver not been in front of me. That's how life is sometimes. We try to cruise straight through life and then frustrating obstacles come and block us in a corner. We get mad at the fact that the obstacles are slowing us down, but we don't realize that trouble could be right on the other side. Often times what we thought was an obstacle, was actually what was saving us from a very costly mistake! Just imagine what type of warfare God's grace has protected you from.

The beauty of a struggle is the security found in knowing that God has a strategic plan throughout all of the chaos. It really is true that God's grace is sufficient and will carry you through anything you encounter. So when things seem too difficult to handle on your own, just remember that God never intended for you to fight your battles alone. We all sang the song "Jesus Loves Me" when we were kids, but do you sometimes forget the simple principle behind those words? *"Jesus loves me this I know, for the bible tells me so. Little ones do him belong; They are weak, BUT HE IS STRONG."* You can't always do it on your own, you must lean on him!

Sometimes a rough situation is the only thing that will strengthen your character and bring to light the best parts of you that you didn't even know existed. Maybe your rough patch is simply a test, letting you know that you're much stronger, with a whole lot more potential than you're giving yourself credit for. Nobody said life would be perfect. Nobody said you'd always feel capable of carrying such heavy loads, however, sometimes the heavy loads are quite necessary to your development. Just like lifting weights builds physical muscle, struggle builds character, resilience, and strength. Instead of crying and praying that every trial be taken away from you, pray for the tools to conquer each battle head on.

You have to be able to recognize when God is moving. When He's placing you in a certain situation. It's

DANGEROUS to just blindly roam through life. It's foolish to think that everything that's happening isn't connected. Even the bible says "all things work together for the good of those that love the Lord," so think about that when you think your situation is pointless and hard for no reason. You don't build muscle by lifting pillows and feathers. You build muscle by lifting weights and carrying things that have some substance to them. Eventually you can carry what you used to not be able to carry and those weights that used to stop you are now light and easy. So, if you want to get even bigger and stronger you have to up your weight class. That's how life works too.

God gives you only what you can bear. So in order to get you to grow, he has to build your muscle step-by-step. Have you ever wondered why just when things start to get easy, right when you're finally feeling comfortable, life suddenly shakes up, and you're stuck lifting heavy weights again? You think it's because your luck is bad and you can't catch a break, but in reality God has to bring you to another weight class because you've served your purpose at the previous level, and now it's time for him to take you higher. However, he can't let you go higher until he gets you strong enough to handle the obstacles that'll come with that new level. You can even look at it like a video game. When you start on level 1 everything is a lot easier than level 25. I'm sure you candy crush lovers can relate. When you first start playing the game, it is easy and you probably breeze right through it. After a few weeks, you'd think that with as many hours as you've been putting into the game, it should be second nature by now, but it seems to become harder requiring more skill. The closer you get to winning and beating the game the harder it becomes because the prize is only for the strong individuals who worked for it. If it were easy to win nobody would want to play the game. So, if in your current struggle you feel like you're not being compensated for your effort and training, don't get discouraged. This is especially a problem for college grads, who like me, thought that because they have earned that college degree, they should start off on level 10 instead of level 1. In reality if your boss were to hire you right in and put you on level 10, chances are you'd run the company into the ground before you could punch out at night. It would happen in the exact same way you'd lose in that video game if the first level you ever played were the one right before the prize. Starting close to the finish line doesn't mean it's easier to get. Starting too close without the right experience, knowledge, training or wisdom will set you back farther than if you were to start slowly and surely working your way to the top. Stay the course, no matter how hard the struggle. I have always heard that if you wait on God, He will put such divine favor on your life that you'll be cast years down the line ahead of where you would've been. He makes up for what you lost.

We've all heard the term "pressure makes diamonds." While that's very "cute" and memorable, for me personally, it has not always been enough when it came time to speak against those feelings of discouragement. The only thing that really helped me was to look back on all the things and situations I had prayed about in the past. Situations I thought I'd never overcome, people I thought I'd never get through to and feats I thought I'd never accomplish. All of those different things are now past tense and have been conquered, thanks to the Lord. Now, when I'm going through a struggle, I keep this quote from an anonymous source in mind: "If ever you feel doubtful of blessings God has in store, remember that what you have now was once among the things you hoped and prayed for!"

There is power to be gained from your struggle, and that power is your testimony. Once you are blessed enough to be brought out of your hard times, it is then up to you to share with others how you were able to get through it. We overcome by the words of our testimonies (Revelation 12:11). One person's ability to be victorious is almost always an indirect result of someone else's story. When we see others accomplish or overcome something similar to where we currently find ourselves, their strength, endurance, and accomplishments can serve as a secondary push in our own lives. If you give up too soon, not only are you hurting yourself, but you are also potentially blocking the domino effect that was supposed to subsequently follow. Whatever you do, keep pushing! Keep moving forward. Never give up on yourself no matter how tough life gets. Like Kanye West said, "That that don't kill me, can only make me stronger."

Everything is happening according to God's perfect will and in His divine timing...

"Life is a journey,
Not a destination,
There are no mistakes,
Just chances we've taken.
Lay down your regrets, cause all we have is now" – **India Arie**

According to the M.A.S.H. game results played in my 8th grade Algebra class, by age 24 I'd be married to J-Boog of B2K, with one kid and another on the way, in school to be a pediatrician, driving a BMW, living in a mansion, with a puppy named D.O.G. It's safe to say that didn't go as predicted. Life in the ten years since then has taken me on a journey that the 14-year-old me could have never imagined. That very journey has made me who I am today.

The struggle and the journey coincide. What I mean is, you don't really get one without the other. If you think your journey is going to be free from trouble, then you might want to think again. Different things may determine everyone's idea of "making it" through their journey. For some it is defined by success in the workplace. For others having a family or leaving a legacy defines it. Whatever the case may be, the purpose of the journey is to develop you into everything God created you to be, in order to be most effective at that destination. It won't happen overnight. As a matter of fact, it'll take you your whole life to complete everything God has put you on Earth to do. Every day you wake up is another opportunity for you to continue along your journey; to push forward through to your destiny and live out your purpose. A day is much deeper than just another twenty-four hours. The journey is like a trip through life, or through a season of your life. The problem for most, however, is enjoying the ride.

All throughout college I couldn't wait to graduate. To get out into the real world and finally be free from books, studying, exams; all of which felt like captivity to me. If I had a paid vacation day now for every time I brushed someone off telling me, "Don't rush through college. Take your time. The adult world isn't all it seems," then I'd be on my way to a long vacation in Dubai. Hindsight is always better, right?

Immediately after graduation, I got a job working at a nursing home and the realities of the real world began to set in. Strict schedules, following someone else's daily orders (and dropping those orders at the request of someone else's more immediate need), and then trying to remember what you were doing before you were interrupted. Oh did I mention health insurance, income taxes, student loan repayments, life insurance, death of the refund check, payday every two weeks, but still more broke than I was in college. No more after class nap, no more friends living down the street or college-town fun, and the reality that "what I want to be when I grow up" is no longer a question of the future, but instead a harsh reality of what my life has now succumbed to. Are you out of breath from reading all of that? I'm tired just thinking about it. It took me a long time to adjust to the "9-to-5 life" for those very reasons. It placed me in an unfamiliar, thus uncomfortable, environment. Not to mention, it was a job that did not require my degree, nor pay the amount of money a recent college graduate would hope or expect to see (or so I thought).

I was so focused on how much better I could be doing and feeling sorry for myself, I couldn't even see the blessing in front of me. I had a job in the medical field, where I could gain experience, network, and learn from more experienced individuals all at the young age of 23. It was at this job that I realized that a college degree does not make you a know-it-all, nor does it necessarily make you superior in the workplace. Despite whatever degree you may have earned, there is always someone you can learn from. Even with school experience, you may be required to work your way up the totem pole. Never be too prideful, humility is key.

Another great thing about me landing that job was that it opened my eyes and made me realize that getting older is inevitable. So, now the words "life is short" mean even more to me. I always thought of it as meaning, life is short because you never know when someone will die, but now I see that somebody doesn't have to be dead in a physical sense to be gone. Some people in that nursing home were in their 90s, while some were in their 50s and 60s. You never know how long you're going to have your loved ones around and in their right minds. It broke my heart every day to see these elderly people who were alive, but couldn't do anymore for themselves than two-year-old babies. It taught me to appreciate my family members while they're still young and alert. It reinforced the fact that I need to accomplish all I can while I'm able! We have to stop living like we've got all the time in the world. Every single day is important; every single hour is crucial.

Above all, what this job did for me is something that I will be forever grateful for. It will probably shock a lot of people to read this; however, what I'm most appreciative of is the fact that it exposed me to a world I had always dreamt of being a part of, and in return showed me just how much it actually wasn't for me. Yep, you read that right.

For the first time in my life, it made me restless and uncomfortable about the future. I finally stopped to think about what BRITTNEY actually wanted to do every day for the rest of her life. Sure, college is all about prepping for the future, but there is nothing like working a job that limits your full potential that will ignite the fire inside that you need to go after your passion. Complacency and comfort breed nothing but average behavior and less than perfect results. It was during this uncomfortable period of my life that I went through what I'll call the *post grad identity crisis.* How does one go to school for five years, earn a degree and plan a life based on a career you have no interest in? Easy—you don't think about it. Well at least I didn't. At a young age, I got settled into the idea of what I wanted, who everyone knew me to be, that I couldn't even see beyond it. I was on auto-pilot and didn't even realize it. I didn't see anything wrong with it, because it was me, or so I thought. Up until that point, my mind couldn't even comprehend being anything other than a physician. And suddenly, it was the last thing I wanted to be. Something just wasn’t sitting well with me and deep down in my spirit it felt like everything was changing. What I didn’t realize was that everything in me wasn’t changing, but instead everything that God placed inside of me was bursting to get out.

How many times do we do this? Get so caught up in an identity that we don't even realize is not us? I was livid. Mad at myself for not realizing this sooner. Disappointed that I’d “wasted” all that time in college on a degree that I suddenly KNEW deep down inside I didn’t want to use. I can’t even describe to you how I knew. It was just instinct. It wasn’t because I didn’t like my medical field job that I decided to change my whole life around, it just so happens that God revealed it to me that way. My doubts about the medical field being right for me came long before I started that job. However, I believe that God knew I’d live a life of doubt and regret had I never gotten that opportunity to wear scrubs to work and be of aid to the sick and in need. It was exactly what I *thought* I wanted; yet I was completely unfulfilled with the idea of moving forward in the field.

I prayed and prayed and prayed that God would show me the way and give me a sign or sense of direction. Unfortunately, nothing seemed to bounce out at me, and I was more confused than ever. I still had no idea what I was going to do with my life career wise, and everything in my life seemed to be falling apart.

I've realized that in order to grow and prosper in your own life, you seriously have to be willing to embrace change. It is pretty much the first step to gaining full appreciation of your personal journey. I'm not just talking about changing when it's fun, either. You have to change when you're not fully ready to change. Change when it is vital to your wellbeing, yet compromising to everything you're so comfortable with. That's the type of change that gets you from wishful thinking to actually DOING.

You can't expect what worked for you last season to still work this season. A lawnmower is of no use to you in the winter, and a snow blower isn't useful in the summer (unless you live in Michigan like me, then that's somewhat debatable).

Different seasons of your life require different mindsets, tools, and people. You're a living, changing being and you will outgrow situations, people, jobs, etc. There's nothing wrong with that. It's healthy and it's natural. If you aren't changing you aren't growing or maturing. Keep in mind; it's hard to grow when everything around you is peaches and cream. If you're content with your surroundings, you have little motivation to work for anything better. Why do you think so many successful rappers, singers, athletes, actors and businessmen and women started from close to nothing? It's not because that's where all the golden opportunities lie, but because those are the people that will do whatever it takes to get out of their unpleasant situations. There are some people who are content with just being alive, and others who want to actually LIVE.

Anyway, back to my story. So, like I said, up until then, I had my post graduate plans all set in stone until this idea of a major career change hit me like a bag of bricks. I had it all figured out. I was going to stay at home for a little while, and then move to Atlanta and stay with my best friend Shauntel until I could get a place of my own. Find a job at an Atlanta-area hospital, meanwhile applying to Physician Assistant grad school programs and medical schools in Atlanta and North Carolina. Next, I'd fall in love with a southern gentleman, and never look back. Boy did God have other ideas. I see why people say He laughs at the "plans" we make for ourselves. Instead of living out, what was at the time, my dream, I was struggling to see the light at the end of the tunnel. What would I do for the rest of my life? What career could I choose that would satisfy me? At this point I hadn't been taught much about purpose and how much it can relate to your career goals, so I didn't even understand the importance of keeping God at the forefront of a career decision. Thankfully, it wasn't long before I began to be exposed to such truths!

God has a way of placing the right information in your life at a time when you're most open and vulnerable to receive it. It's never a coincidence that my pastor always delivers a message that seems to be specifically catered to me and what I'm going through, time after time. When the Holy Spirit speaks through someone, to us, suddenly our antennas are fully charged, and every message, word and scripture we hear seems to tie into what we are going through. For me, everything seemed to relate to the importance of discovering one's purpose in life and living to your greatest potential. That was nothing but God and the workings of the Holy Spirit! Pay attention to those "ah-ha" moments! They could potentially change your life.

What happened next is history. I began to pay closer attention to my surroundings, searching for the lesson in every situation. I was eager to figure out why God had me at each particular stage in my life, so that I could be sure to gain the most out of every experience. I no longer began to look at experiences for just what they were at the surface, but how they could make me better. This was an especially useful positive thinking tool to have as I jumped around from three different jobs in my first year out of school (exactly what they tell you NOT to do). I couldn't listen to the people who told me what I was doing wasn't a good idea. The people that tried to make me question whether or not I should stick to my first idea of medical school. To them it didn't seem very wise or stable of me to hop from my first job at a nursing home, to a non-profit debt relief call center, and then finally to a high school registrar position. It didn't make sense to the normal eye. However, I knew that I was right where God needed me to be. I knew that every step of the way he was walking me through a different part of my journey to my destiny. MY Journey. MY destiny. Not anyone else's, meaning it may not look just like EVERYONE else's.

Because I made the conscious effort to soak up knowledge, I was able to see the calm behind the chaotic storm that comes with the journey towards honing in on your true passion. I made the decision to "LIVE and not just exist," as O. Wilde stated. When you decide you really want to LIVE that's when faith comes into the picture.

Faith is what successfully takes you from one stage of the journey to the next. It's easy to trust God when you're sitting in the comfort of your own normality's, but will you trust Him when he leads you to shake some things up? Or will you be too consumed with worry to move? Faith without works is dead, and an opportunity presented but not taken becomes a tragic case of "what if." You absolutely cannot appreciate the "journey" without faith. Without faith, the journey is more like a shackled prison walk towards freedom. Hoping and wishing that one-day it'd all make sense. That one day it'll all pay off. Who wants to live like that? Why not learn to take full advantage of the life lessons along the way. I don't know about everyone else, but if I have to go through unpleasant times whether it be a relationship or friendship gone sour, a job I hate, a period of financial strain, etc., I want to at least come out of it with some valuable insight.

I don't want anything I go through to have been in vain. You've just got to open your eyes. Sounds simple, right? Only if you have the faith to believe that there really is a lesson in every hardship, and that God really is there and fully capable of seeing you through. You've got to have faith that everything isn't what it seems and that the victory will soon be yours! It's so hard for people to have faith when it comes to their life's journey because society teaches us that we are to be in full control in order to be successful. They leave little room for us to be uncertain about the individual steps, yet confident in the master plan.

That's how I look at my life and how faith ties into it. No, I don't know how everything will tie together or how it'll all work out, but I know without a doubt that God can make it all happen. I know that God opens doors that no man can shut (Revelation 3:7), and that he is able to do exceedingly and abundantly above all I could ever ask or think (Ephesians 3:20). I look at it like this: Most of the time we tend to only have partial faith. We say, "I trust that God knows all and He will take care of everything," but our actions say otherwise. When most people get on an airplane they don't have a parachute, lifejacket, rope, ladder, etc. in their carry-on bag. They get on the plane with complete trust and faith that the pilot knows what he is doing, and IF something were to go wrong, they trust that the staff is fully equipped to save them. So how can we say we really trust God if we constantly make our own backup plans and agendas "just in case" what God says doesn't happen the way we THINK it should. When the pilot says "it's now safe to take off your seatbelts" while in the air, how many of us stop and say, "Well maybe I can take off my seatbelt, but let me just handcuff myself to the seat just in case it gets a little rocky in here?" Nobody! So when God says, "Stop taking matters into your own hands, and let me be your pilot, let my word be your seatbelt, why are we so reluctant to listen?" You don't have to fully understand it. We don't know where the pilot got his license, or if he knows which buttons to push on the control panel, but we trust him enough to get on that plane.

Even when you don't understand how it's all going to work out, remember that the Bible says that faith the size of a mustard seed is all you need. Trust God. Trust the Journey!

You have to have something to live for...
something bigger than yourself.

"The gift God gave to you,
Give it back to him,
For the gift, it will make room- position,
for great men to see you.
The gift it looks good on you." – ***Donald Lawrence***

To go after one's dreams is unfortunately something most will only have the courage to do while they're sound asleep. The brave person who chooses to pursue such dreams while awake and conscious is a person whose autobiography reads of exhilarating tales of having lived with no regrets, told via a captivating plot, and a happier ending. Simply put, those who go after their dreams are more likely to live a fulfilling life than those who never dared to try. You can never be too scared to dream. A failed dream leaves behind a lesson learned, while a dream never explored leaves behind the guilt of what could have been.

I distinctly remember the day I decided to dream bigger, smarter, and better. It was May 31, 2013. I had just cried, *real tears*, to my parents a few weeks before about how I felt the medical field might not be for me after all. I'd been researching every career imaginable in my field of study and nothing seemed interesting to me. What a complete bummer that was. My parents told me to pray on it and ask God to give me some direction. They also asked me what it was I could see myself doing every day. I started thinking about what I like to do. What excites me, what gets me going, and what I'd like to help change. After much thought and prayer a few good ideas began to surface. I liked to help people. I liked to inspire others. I liked to mentor younger generations. I liked to write. I went to my mom and told her that I felt like my dream job didn't exist. I'll never forget her response. "Then create it." My dad agreed!

Sometimes all you need is for someone to speak life into you like that. For someone to tell you it's okay to be uncertain, but that it's better to go after your thoughts and goals than to live a life of regrets and "what ifs?" That was all the momentum I needed to push forward just a little bit. So back to May 31st, I emailed my friend/sister, Marchelle, and told her about an idea to form some type of platform to inspire people and mentor younger girls. Her response was filled with encouragement and excitement! Two days later, June 2nd, Pastor Glenn, gave a dynamic word about how he believed that God would be giving us ideas that would flourish and lead us to success beyond our wildest dreams. That was confirmation directly to me that my ideas would soon become a reality. Please realize that at this point, I wasn't even living in Grand Rapids anymore, as I had moved back home one month prior, after graduation. So being there that day was divinely orchestrated. I remember sewing a financial seed (an offering given with expectation) during the service, as a direct response to the message under the instruction of Pastor Glenn. I knew that this was MY TIME to make some power moves. Over the next few days I thought and prayed endlessly on what exactly God was showing me. He began to show me bits and pieces of the big picture and I was eager, yet somewhat mind blown.

Something told me to call my friend Erikka after work about a week later and tell her my idea. That "something" was definitely the Holy Spirit, because what followed was divine.

Erikka and I, along with ten other ambitious and supportive women went on to establish MISSion.31

Incorporated, a non-profit mentoring group for young ladies in grades 6-12. I was VERY iffy about how I was going to make it work, but God provided peace and provision to support my vision. I have no background or training in non-profit administration. One could say that I don't even have the least bit of formal knowledge of what it takes to start and run a functioning business. Sure I'd run a lemonade stand and sold Girl Scout cookies when I was a kid. I'd even had a little leadership experience from having been the president of my sorority's chapter on campus, but as far as starting a business from the ground up, I had no knowledge whatsoever. I learned chemistry and biology in college, and here now God wants me to run a business? That's a leap of faith, I kid you not.

So no, I may not have all the knowledge, but what I do have, is drive, ambition, a willingness to learn, and great great GREAT people around me. God strategically placed every single person on our executive board for a specific reason. Nobody was brought on board by accident or for show, but because they had something unique and valuable to offer. In fact, every department head one could possibly need was covered due to the natural talents and educational skills of my team. I didn't have to outsource skilled help, because God delivered them right to my doorstep. From programming, website development, public relations and branding, human resources, videography, educators, and networking connections, MISSion.31's executive board has someone for it all. There is something powerful about letting God lead you in the decision of who to bring in to help you build your dreams.

Even with all of that talent, the task of building a business from the ground up was very challenging at times. Trial and error is most definitely the best way to describe it. In my head, I thought it would be easy and would just spring off the ground and run full force right away. Wrong. Wrong. Wrong. While the vision came to life rather quickly thanks to the hard work and support of the entire executive board and volunteers, we still hit bump after bump in the road of development. Despite the bumps and delays, we were still able to establish ourselves as an up-and-coming positive movement. We created the Mission IMpossible movement to encourage others to turn what some deem impossible into the possible. Hundreds of people bought Mission IMpossible t-shirts and provided the support that we so greatly needed.

Eventually, we were able to select our very first group of mentors and mentees and officially launch the mentoring component of our program. Coincidently, exactly one year from the day I first decided to DREAM BIG, on May 31, 2014, MISSion.31 held our first Mentor Orientation. Our mentors were trained by a highly skilled prevention specialist (who also is a member of our board.), and then paired up with their younger mentees. I was utterly amazed when I stood back and watched how what was once just a thought in my head (and heart), actually come alive. Words cannot explain what it feels like to see your dreams come true, even if it is just in the beginning stages. Because I took that leap of faith to step outside the box, I know that the possibilities of what it will evolve into are beyond endless. Because I took that leap of faith, countless lives will be changed for generations to come. What seems to you like a scary and impossible task could be the purpose-filled dream given to you to impact the world and kingdom of God.

I'm the type of girl who is big on signs and symbolism. Not the spooky kind, but the signs from God that let me know he's with me every step of the way. I was amazed at the "coincidence" that my idea started on May 31, 2013, and then such a monumental day for our organization occurred exactly one year later. So imagine how mind boggled I was when my mother pointed out to me that those days occurred on the 31st of the month... MISSion.31... **31.** All I could say was, "I hear you God, and I will continue to do everything that I can to lead this organization." Not only does that show that God will reassure you along the way, but it reassured me that everything happens in divine order according to His timing. You cannot rush God. You can try all you want, but he has the final say-so of how and when things play out. Just do your part and in due time everything will work out. I thought I was going to create a brand new business, have mentors willing to volunteer and mentees ready for a mentor all within a matter of months. That's how we are sometimes with our own dreams. Because WE know how good they have the potential to be, we expect everyone around us to see it as well, and things to flow effortlessly. Life just doesn't work that way, and it's for our own good that it doesn't. If your blessings come to you before you're equipped to handle them, you run the risk of ruining it all before you can really get started. God's timing is your protection, trust it.

For years I dreamt of writing a book. I knew that I had something in my spirit to share with the world, but I couldn't figure out how to say it. So, I didn't write one. However, that burning desire inside of me never went away, no matter how much I ignored it. When I was bored and needed something to do, the thought of sitting down and starting my first book often crossed my mind, but I always talked myself out of it. Many of us do the exact same things when it comes to some of the great ideas and visions we have. Unfortunately, a large majority of people will never act on their dreams. They'll blame it on not having enough time, or not knowing how to make it happen. I think one of the worst things that can happen to a person is to die without attempting to follow their true passion and accomplish their wildest dreams.

Now that you know a little bit about my dreams, I'm going to break it down further so that you are able to better see how this concept can play out in your own life. So, let's examine the basis of a **dream** for a moment. Webster's dictionary defines a dream as "a strongly desired goal or purpose." Well, what is a purpose? A purpose is "the reason for which something is done or created, or for which something exists." Now, let's think about who created that dream, which is connected to that purpose, that is your reason for walking this earth? *God*. God gave you the dream so that you could follow your purpose. That's right, your purpose in life is not decided or created by your own thoughts. God created you for a purpose before you were even born. A car isn't manufactured by Ford, Chrysler, or BMW so that it can one day decide that maybe, just maybe, it would like to be able to drive people around. Before a car is a car, it is a bunch of individual parts that are put together for the sole purpose of becoming a vehicle. That's similar to how God works in our lives. We aren't placed here on Earth for no reason, just to lollygag around and hopefully someday figure out a way to make our lives worthwhile. We are born to live out a certain plan God has for us. That plan, that purpose, is something that we must discover, by seeking the only One who created it. This is why it is so important to truly figure out who you are because without knowing WHO you are, you won't be able to figure out WHAT you're supposed to do.

You want God to reveal your purpose? Stop talking so much. I know, I know, we love to talk! It's a good thing, but sometimes you have to stop telling God what you want Him to do, long enough for Him to show you what he needs you do to. As long as you're trying to take control, and as long as you have this well planned out agenda, without first consulting with your creator, you'll never be able to hear what He made you for.

One of the first steps to finding your purpose in life is to understand the fact that you did not create it. You were created with a purpose to live out a purpose. A vacuum cleaner is created with the purpose of sucking up dirt, dust, and debris that people can't really get up by hand. A vacuum is not created to cut the grass or plow a snow-covered driveway. As much as you may want your vacuum cleaner to mop your floor, it never will. Sure it may do an okay job of getting it clean, but it's still not a mop. As much as your mother may want you to be a lawyer, and as decent (or not so decent) your grades may be in your political science classes, if you weren't created to be a lawyer, then it's still not your purpose. You may even succeed in becoming a lawyer and do a great job at it, and help effect the world while you're at it. Trust me, I've seen folks vacuum their kitchen floors. Both realistically and hypothetically speaking.

You've probably heard the quote by Albert Einstein that states, "Everybody is a genius. But if you judge a fish by its ability to climb a tree, it will live its whole life believing that it is stupid." So, all that I'm really saying is, if you judge a vacuum on it's capability to give you spotless shiny kitchen floors, then you may feel like something's missing from the vacuum, like it just isn't good enough. You'll never realize that in the right environment, serving the right purpose, living out its creative function, it can clean carpets better than any tool in your house. That's EXACTLY how you are, when you're stuck operating in an environment that doesn't correlate to where God created you to be. You may feel frustrated, overwhelmed, or invaluable. It's not that you're not good enough, talented enough, or smart enough. It just simply may not be the area God naturally gifted you in. It doesn't matter how untalented you think you are, I guarantee you, God has placed a unique gift inside of you.

Your purpose is tied into your natural gifts. It involves doing what you are usually able to do rather effortlessly (so to speak), that is not so easy for others. If you think about what you love to do, or what you'd do every day even if money wasn't a factor, chances are your purpose is tied up somewhere in that realm. When I started to figure out different aspects of my purpose, I realized that God placed the exact tools inside of me at a very young age. When I was three years old I had countless books memorized word for word. I was too young to actually read a book, but nobody would know it from how well I could recite them from cover to cover. A few years later, I was writing my own stories. I never thought much of it when I was younger, as I was just doing it for fun. God placed the gift of writing inside me, long before I knew I would publish a book.

When I was about 10 years old I ran my own card-making business. My family didn't own a computer or printer at the time, but what we did have was a little word processor, which is something like a fancy typewriter. I figured out how to print double-sided greeting cards, and then hustled them out to my family members. The cards weren't very professional looking, but people bought them because they respected my young grind.

I also started a backyard cheerleading team when I was in 8th grade, because I couldn't try out for my middle school team due to time conflict. I gathered up a few friends for the team and solicited the help of a coach (my aunt Keni). It didn't last too long, given that we didn't have any sports teams to actually cheer for, but you can't knock a girl for trying.

Do you see where I'm going with this? The skills I thought I lacked to get started on the mission God has for my life, have actually been embedded in me all along, even when I didn't realize so. I've always been a writer, a visionary, and an entrepreneur. What have you always been great at? What are you naturally gifted to do?

Let's fast forward a bit and tackle the question you might have next. What do you do when God reveals your purpose? What do you do if once you realize that he has given you this gift, you still feel undeserving of receiving it? You feel like you don't have the tools to accomplish it, or maybe you're just scared. How do you move forward? Well, first let's talk about a gift.

Romans 12:6 says "we have different gifts, according to the grace that is given to us." The definition of the word gift is "something bestowed or acquired without any particular effort by the recipient; not earned." Two key words stood out to me in that scripture and definition. Grace and Given. The definition of Grace is "manifestation of favor." The word given means "executed and delivered."

So, basically that scripture in Romans tells us that a gift is something that requires little to no effort to obtain, because you are favored enough to receive it. You are right, you don't deserve it, but it's still yours. Thanks to favor it's already been delivered. Not ordered. Not on its way. It is in your possession! Use it, with confidence. Don't question how you got it, or if God meant to give it to you. He makes no mistakes. It's yours!

God gives us dreams, visions and desires, as a means to serve as a glimpse of the ultimate plan we must follow to serve our purpose. In the Old Testament of the Bible,

God presented a dream to many people in order to show them what they would one day accomplish.

Whenever He provided the vision, He always provided prearranged steps for it to transpire. God gave Noah the dream to build an ark and gave him specific directions to make it happen. Noah was the only person on earth who could live out the purpose God had for him. In order for him to live out his purpose, he had to dream first.

The same thing happened with Abraham. Abraham was given the desire to be a father. He then had a dream orchestrated by God that not only informed him that he'd be a father, but a father of many nations. This dream was given to him when he and his wife were well past the age of childbearing. Unqualified, one may say. God however, specializes in using exactly whom the world deems unqualified.

Just look at young David slaying the 9.5-foot tall giant, Goliath. Or Peter, Andrew, James and John—regular fishermen, turned right hand men to Jesus, the Savior of the world. I can't forget Rahab, a woman who was both a prostitute and a Canaanite, the Israelites arch enemies. She hid and protected two Israelites against her own people during an invasion; an unlikely hero she was indeed. Just to tie that in with the last chapter and the significance of the journey, Rahab's future great-grandson was King David, meaning she was an ancestor to Jesus himself.

God will use you despite how ordinary you may think you are, so that when it all plays out, everyone will know that it was God working through you to manifest such greatness. You're never too old, too young, too big, too small, too poor, uneducated, uncultured, or unsaved for God to use you!

So how did I start dreaming bigger? I'm no different than each and every one of you reading this. How did I gather up the courage to step outside my comfort zone and start a non-profit organization, or even write this book? I wouldn't even say I had the courage at first. To this day it honestly terrifies me that so many people are reading my innermost thoughts. However, I made up my mind that I was tired of mediocrity. Tired of thinking about *one day*. I hated the feeling of always wondering when things would finally take off. So I decided to go for it.

A dream without a plan is simply a wish. Wishful thinking often gets us nowhere. Proactive, strategic, effective thinking can build an empire. Everyone deserves his or her own empire! If that means owning your own business or your own practice, then by all means do it! I can only image how many potential life solutions and businesses are DYING in the minds of folks, working day in and day out at the 9 to 5 job that they

HATE! That's no way to live! I'm not even sure you can really call that living. Now, I'm not the one to try and convince everyone in the world to be an entrepreneur. I think it's foolish to think that the only way to be a world-changer is to own your own business. Nobody's business or life, as we know it, could function if everyone was the boss. America wouldn't be America without "Corporate America" and all of the hard workers that play a role in it. You just have to find where exactly you fit into the puzzle. For MANY people, accomplishing your dreams doesn't mean starting something new, but instead making an impact in an infrastructure that already exists. For MANY other people, accomplishing your goals means being a pioneer to something NEW and unheard of. It means starting a company and being your own boss. Either way, find your place and become the absolute best at it that you possibly can. Leave a legacy! Your legacy is an empire in and of itself because it will inspire someone, who will then inspire someone else. Now that is living.

You could have the biggest dreams, ideas, and visions in the world, but without execution, they're just going to sit there in your head, and in your head they are as good as dead. Sure they're keeping you alive, giving you an inkling of hope to hold onto. But God didn't give you your dreams for you to daydream about them all day. He gave them to you because He trusted you to deliver them to the world. He wants to use you to show the world what He can do.

I saw a post on Instagram one day that really inspired me. It said something to the effect of never giving up on your dreams. It stated that Walt Disney was fired from his job working for a newspaper because the company felt his ideas lacked creativity and originality. It also stated that Oprah Winfrey was asked to step down from her position as a news anchor because producers felt she wasn't really fit for television. Another part that amazed me was when it said that at one point Steve Jobs was fired from the very company he started. Imagine what would have happened if Walt Disney decided not to pursue his crazy idea of drawing a talking mouse. Or if Oprah Winfrey got a job working in retail, because she thought that pursuing a career in television would be too hard and time consuming? Imagine how different YOUR life would be had Steve Jobs thought that continuing to push and develop his software system was pointless seeing that Bill Gates already had the market covered. Say goodbye to the iPhone. The world would have been very different had these folks not acted on their dreams and visions no matter how crazy they must have seemed at the time. You are no different than those three world-changers. The only difference between them and you right now is a plan, ambition and making the right connections.

You need to create a distinct plan to bring your dream to life. So many people's dreams die because they don't develop a plan to ensure the proper steps are followed. You can't just wish something into happening, you have to ACT! "Write the vision; make it plain" says Habakkuk 2:2, which continues on to read "For still the vision awaits its appointed time; it hastens to the end—it will not lie. If it seems slow, wait for it; it will surely come; it will not delay." What does that mean to me? It's simple. Say your dreams aloud. Say them for exactly what they are. Be specific with your prayers. Then, patiently wait, no matter how long it takes. If God gave you the dream, it'll happen, for sure. Just do what you can on this side of heaven to get ready, and God will surely handle the rest from his side. Favor, Mercy, Divine Connections, Grace, Dominion, Power and Authority. He'll give you whatever it is that you need.

Everybody won't always be happy for you. Everyone may not get as excited about your dreams as you are and everyone most certainly won't always agree with your decisions. And you know what? That's perfectly fine. God didn't give them your vision for a reason. He gave it to you because it is yours. You have to learn to move off your own support alone. I love the song "Encourage Yourself" sung by the Tri City Singers because sometimes that's exactly what you have to do. You may have to be your own teammate, but just find peace in knowing that God is the ultimate coach who will never let you lose. You just have to be willing to listen and follow His plays and instructions.

In order for any great plan to work, you must have ambition. You have to be willing to work against all odds, to prove all naysayers wrong, and to bounce back even harder when doors of opportunity are slammed in your face. The space between a dream and a success story is filled with an abundance of adversities one has overcome.

When you dream and come up with a plan to make that dream come true, prepare as if your golden opportunity will be presented to you tomorrow morning. Too many of us are waiting until it's too late to start getting prepared! That is the whole purpose of preparing, to get ready *ahead of time,* even when it doesn't seem like its time.

Getting ready when it doesn't seem like you have much of a reason to is another premise of faith. Had Noah waited until he saw rain coming down to get ready to build the ark, he would have drowned. If you wait until someone tells you "yes" to start getting ready, you will become overwhelmed. You'll drown in regret when your opportunity passes you by for the person who took the time to get ready and beat you to the punch.

If your dream is to start a business, then draft a business plan. If your dream is to write a book, start listing chapters and ideas. If your dream is to go to college, start studying and fill out an application. You don't want to miss out on your success story because you were too lazy or scared to prepare. You MUST WORK FOR IT. Success does not fall into your lap. It takes hard work. It takes resilience. It takes tenacity. It takes a blatant disregard for FEAR. So if you have a dream, something you think about day in and day out, Do It! Don't let your whole life pass you by because you were waiting for the perfect time to get started. No matter what, we can almost always convince ourselves that we just need one more day, six more months, one more year to get ourselves ready. Chances are, you'll never feel fully prepared, so if that's what you're waiting on, you may never move forward. "Prepare your work outside; get everything ready for yourself in the field, and after that build your house" (Proverbs 24:27).

Now, once you've zoned in on your golden idea, the dream you want to nurture and deliver to the world, and are comfortable enough to move in it, the real work begins. It's now imperative that you protect your dream by any means necessary, even against yourself. You've got to make it a point to check yourself in a major way about one thing in particular: Comparison. It is the thief of joy. Bear with me for a moment as I step on my soapbox.

I've struggled with comparison a lot. Especially once I approached the one-year anniversary of my graduation from college. Everyone around me was falling in love, moving up the totem pole in their careers, or graduating with master's degrees. It felt like everyone else was moving forward, except me. In school, I studied harder than almost everyone I knew. My books were bigger, my homework was harder, my fun time was much more limited. Then after college, it seemed like everyone's careers were soaring, while I bounced from job to job, industry to industry. IT JUST DIDN'T MAKE SENSE TO ME. I mean, don't get me wrong, I knew that I had a SEED in the ground. I knew that eventually my latter would be greater, that everything would make sense, that my tests would be testimonies, and that "some guy would be so blessed to have me one day..." right? Okay yeah, but what about now? It is so hard to consciously TRY to do right, when everyone around you is doing the absolute opposite, and it seems like they're the ones winning. It was like the harder I tried to walk in the will of God, the more things just didn't add up. That's the thing about walking a Christian walk though; nobody ever said that abandoning yourself was easy. In fact it's hard work! The bible states that we will NEVER see the righteous forsaken (Psalm 37:25). So, with that in mind, I continue to seek his will for my life and remain open minded for what is to come.

I have realized that one of the reasons I get knocked completely off my square is when I start looking around too much. Looking around at what everyone else is doing, how they're succeeding, and what's going on in their worlds. Once you start looking, it's in your human nature to start comparing. Once you start comparing, it is so easy to either start doubting yourself, coveting, competing, or become jealous. All four of which can be detrimental to what you have going for yourself. Here's why;

1. When you **doubt** yourself because someone else is doing it better, you belittle your own credibility and diminish your potential.
2. The bible lists **coveting** as one of 10 MOST important things we should not do. It's a commandment, meaning it's a big deal — and it is for our own good, because God himself said it. If you're too busy trying to fit yourself into someone else's story, you'll never be the star of your own. Everyone's journey through life is different. Just because they got there faster, doesn't mean their story is any better than yours, and it certainly doesn't mean yours won't end just as great.
3. The world love scales. Grading scales. Physical scales, ratings etc. They'll do anything to measure you against others. Friendly **competition** is healthy. What's not so great is when you become so engulfed in looking better or doing it better than the next, that you forget what it is you're supposed to be doing and why

you're doing it. We've all seen it happen before. When something that should be great is clouded by all the daily "shade" being thrown on the opponent. People stop looking at what you actually have going on because they can't see past the drama.

4. There will always be someone out there with something you want. If you become too consumed with that fact, you'll be jealous of everything and everyone, every single day. **Jealousy** is a concept that shouldn't make much sense when you're a firm believer in God. You see, God has more than enough blessings to go around. His supply is in no way limited. Your blessing has your name on it and nobody in the world can change that. So there's no reason to hate on someone else's success. Plus, it's just not cute.

So stay focused and MIND YOUR BUSINESS. Stay in your lane as they say. You can't focus on what needs to be done over here, if you keep looking over there! You have to be secure in the fact that God has a path for your life, and a space for your dream to flourish!

I hope this chapter has motivated you to follow whatever dream(s) you may have. Or at least sparked the fire that will encourage you to start thinking about what it is you want to accomplish. Whatever it is, make sure you do it BIG. Sure you may have to start small, but never let anything limit how big and creative your dreams can be. You're important and as Academy Award Winning Actress, Lupita Nyongo stated, "Your dreams are valid." I think about my dreams all day. I'm almost always plotting. I just feel like there's so much of the world to see than what most people take advantage of. There are so many lives to touch. I just can't settle for the norm, my soul won't let me do it. If I have to live wondering what could've happened, I'll regret it forever.

The passion for everything that makes up what I want to ultimately do is like a volcano stirring up in my mind. Consequently, I indulge in everything involved in the process of accomplishing my goals. I'm constantly researching how people before me got to where they are today; or what they were doing at my age. I'm always exploring various strategies and learning who's who in the industry I want to be a part of. I am determined and willing to work and commit. I've made a promise to myself to do everything in my power to make it. Then when that's not enough, God's amazing grace will take me the rest of the way.

So once you decide to go for it, as you should, stay strong and stay encouraged. Following dreams is not for the weak-hearted, the easily discouraged or dismayed. It is not for the content, or easily satisfied. Following dreams is for the wild and crazy. For the fearless, ambitious warrior who isn't scared of the word "no." The opportunist, who isn't depressed at the site of a closed door, but views it as an opportunity to make a grand entrance by climbing through the window. Dreamers take risks. Dreamers don't give up. Dreamers win.

A Purpose Driven Dreamer's Creed

"In my heart I know I that I am on assignment. An assignment that is not of this world, but of God. I also know that faith comes by hearing the word of God...and that faith without action is not faith. I was born to be GREAT, but I cannot reach greatness as long as I am comfortable with being average. There are too many people living comfortably uncomfortable lives. I choose not to be one of them. In order to see extraordinary results, I must follow the uncommon recipe. When I continue to do what society deems normal, I'll only receive what society deems okay. I want success that is not of this world. I want success covered in God's blessings. I choose to dream! I choose to take action on my dream. Nobody on this earth can stop me no matter how hard they try. The devil has no power over my life, nor my dreams, goals, and ambitions. I choose to live greater! I am a purpose-driven dreamer."

Epiphany 8

You are who you constantly say you are.
You have what you constantly talk about.

"Cause I am a Superwoman
Yes I am, yes she is
Still when I'm a mess, I still put on a vest
With a S on my chest
Oh yes, I'm a Superwoman" - ***Alicia Keys***

Your words are some of the most powerful tools you have possession of. "Life and death lie in the power of your tongue" (Proverbs 18:21). Meaning your words truly do have a significant influence in the way your life ends up. One of the biggest lies we're told as a child is "sticks and stones may break my bones, but words may never hurt me."

Words have the power to kill, but they also have the power to create and revive. When people say you have the ability to create your own reality, they are telling the truth. Think about when you were a little kid and wanted to play hooky to get out of going to school. Did you ever lie and tell your parents you were too sick to go school, and then ended up actually feeling not so well? What about now that you're older? When someone at work asks how you're doing today and you constantly say, "I'm tired," don't you actually feel tired when you say it? Here's one that will really hit home with a lot of you. After a break up, or when something sad happens, if someone asks you to talk about it, if you're honest and tell them that you're very upset and sad, you may begin to produce actual tears. Whereas, if you tell them everything's fine, you're less likely to lose your cool in front of them. All of these examples show the power words and thoughts have on your body's reactions.

We are emotional beings, women especially. Words trigger emotions and emotions then trigger everything else. If you continue to speak something negative into existence, eventually your mind and body will follow along. Imagine trying to run a mile outside while yelling, "I'm fat, slow and out of shape!" You probably won't perform as well as someone running the same distance yelling, "I am the fastest woman in the whole world! I'm young and fit!" If you disagree, why don't you go try it out for yourself! To a certain extent, you can gain control of your life simply by filtering the thoughts and words you allow your mind to speak and accept. Psych yourself out. Fake it until you make. Speak your reality until your reality is real! It's just that simple. The bible says in Proverbs 23:7, "For so a man thinketh, so is he." By controlling what thoughts and words you speak, you control what you focus on and what you respond to! Words and thoughts have so much power. The way we look at a situation is ultimately how that situation will be.

You have to be like the little engine that could and say "I think I can, I think I can" until you start to reap the benefits of your sacrifice. Realize that your biggest critic is the one inside of you. Once you are fully convinced that you are capable of accomplishing something, there will be absolutely nothing that anyone could attempt to tell you to get you to disagree. It won't matter how crazy you sound, or how much your present circumstances don't reflect your vision. When you have 100% faith in yourself and an unlimited amount of faith in GOD, there are no limits to what you can accomplish!

Conclusion

I've reached a very humbling place in my life, to say the least. I'm starting to realize that I'm not the one in control. I realize that I can be somewhat of a control freak, and that it irks my soul to let others handle things for me. However, after finding myself at a point in my life where I cannot help myself, I can firmly attest to the fact that God is the one who can turn my current situation around.

I see why they say college and your 20's are a period of self -discovery. I owe everything that I am and ever will be to the lessons I've learned in the past few years. I'm not superwoman, so I promise that if I can recognize and overcome my inner struggles, then so can you. I'm emotional. I get stressed out very easily, and I shut down. However, I've taken the very lessons that I put in this book to transform my weaknesses into my strengths. Life has a way of taking you on trips you didn't pack for, to destinations you didn't plan to show up to, all for the purpose of learning lessons, meeting people, and gaining knowledge that shapes everything that makes up who you are.

When I began to focus in on what was important, everything changed.

My behavior changed, my attitude and outlook on life, my present situation, my worries, the way I spoke, what I tolerated, what I expected. I realized that mistakes happen so that we can hopefully learn from them. If you aren't learning, you'll keep on repeating the cycle. My life as a whole has matured to a much higher level, one where I am able to see that the sky is no longer the limit. In fact, the limit no longer exists if you ask me.

One of my favorite mottos for life simply states: "Have a healthy disregard for the impossible." I'm not sure who originally stated that quote, but I live by it. Meaning that in whatever you do, do it as if the word impossible doesn't exist. Do it as if you cannot fail. Forget any limitations the world may try to tell you exist. No great discoveries in this world came about from people following business as usual. When God created you, He put gifts and abilities inside of you that can be used by you and you only. You are a limited edition model filled with everything you need to be what God has called you to be. It may take experience to perfect the skills. It may take hardships to strengthen your character. It may take time to develop the patience, diligence, work ethic and confidence. But it is the journey that crafts you; the way you grow as a person as you embark upon life's changes; the way your mind develops as a result of successfully making your way through each stage of life as timing calls for. You don't become a doctor in one day. You usually don't make a million dollars in one day either but, if you add up a bunch of "one-days" together it can happen!

The journey is what is most beautiful of all. Life would be such a bore if we knew exactly how the story would unfold from the beginning. There's just something so thrilling about always having another chapter to anticipate, improve upon and dream about. It gives you a reason to always keep pushing for greater. So keep that in mind the next time the going gets tough. Live your daily life with the expectation that God is going to do something GREAT for and through you each and every day. Remember that you are the master of your thoughts and perspective is everything. If you look at the world through dirty lenses and a negative state of mind, it doesn't matter how beautiful the scenery is because you'll never be able to really see it.

My final, and most important epiphany: ***God can take even your ugliest situation and turn it around to be used for his glory***. Your life is a reflection of the way you view your world, what you believe you can accomplish, and who you aspire to be....

Shift your vision to change your reality.

About the Author

Brittney Michelle is a graduate of Grand Valley State University, where she earned a B.S. in Biomedical Sciences. She has since taken a huge detour from her original career aspirations in the medical field to pursue her God-given purpose and passion: inspiring others. She is committed to helping people tap into their fullest potential, as she humbly works to do so herself. Brittney is the founder and CEO of MISSion.31 Incorporated, a non-profit mentoring organization founded upon the principles described in Proverbs 31. MISSion.31 strives to teach, mentor, and inspire young ladies in grades 6-12, so that they can gain the decision-making skills, self-confidence, and support necessary to become the best they can be. It is her dream that one day, she will be able to inspire and encourage people across the world through her organization and written publications.

Made in the USA
Charleston, SC
08 April 2016